What Every Man Should Know

Timeless Truths for Living with Purpose, Strength, and Integrity

Harrison S. Mungal, Ph.D, Psy.D

What Every Man Should Know

Unless otherwise identified, Scripture quotations are from New King James Version of the Bible.

Contact author via email:
hsmungal@hotmail.com
info@agetoage.ca
www.agetoage.ca
www.harrisonmungal.com
www.harrisonmungalbooks.com
Facebook: Harrison Mungal
Twitter: AgeToAgeInc1
LinkedIn: Harrison Mungal, Ph.D., PsyD
YouTube: Harrison Mungal
Phone: 905-533-1334

ABOUT *the* AUTHOR

Harrison Sharma Mungal, BTh, MCC, MSW, PhD, PsyD

Dr. Mungal is a devoted therapist with a background in mental health and clinical psychology, driven by a genuine passion for life and the well-being of those under his care. With an impressive literary portfolio comprising over 50 books and a seasoned public speaking career that has reached audiences in over 53 nations, he brings a wealth of knowledge and skills to his practice.

Alongside his professional accomplishments, Dr. Mungal places a high value on family, with a successful marriage of over 35 years, seven children, and multiple grandchildren. In addition to his clinical practice, Dr. Mungal and his wife have played pivotal roles in church planting, pastoral ministry, and missionary work, even during the challenging times of the Cold War in Croatia from 1994-1997. They have nurtured congregations, established churches, and served as missionaries, demonstrating a deep commitment to spreading the gospel. Their dedication extended to running a Bible college, Metro Bible College, for over a decade before transitioning into mental health and addictions counselling.

Dr. Mungal is widely respected for his unique ability to blend biblical principles with scientific insights, adding a distinctive "psychology twist" to his therapeutic approach. He explained God made us Body, Soul (mind, will and emotions) and Spirit. As much as people need support physically and spiritually, "the soul is where people are wounded and is in need of healing." His expertise has been sought after by various media outlets, including appearances on television programs including 700 Clubs Canada and 100 Huntly St. He has also been invited to speak at prestigious institutions such as the Attorney General of Canada, police departments, hospitals, community agencies, and churches. His contributions have earned him accolades and recognition from local authorities, police departments, mayors, community leaders, and countless families.

With over 21 years of experience in mental health, psychiatry, and psychology, coupled with over four decades dedicated to teaching and preaching the gospel, Dr. Mungal possesses a wealth of expertise in both fields. His educational background is equally impressive, with a Christian Leadership Certificate, a Ministerial Diploma from two years of Bible College, a bachelor's degree in Theology, two master's degrees (in Counselling and Social Work), and two doctorate degrees (in Social Work and Clinical Psychology).

In summary, Dr. Mungal's journey is a testament to his unwavering commitment to serving others, integrating his faith with his professional expertise to make a positive impact in the lives of countless individuals, couples, and families. His multifaceted career reflects a deep sense of purpose and a profound dedication to promoting holistic healing and spiritual growth.

Table of Contents

INTRODUCTION

What Every Man Should Know – Timeless Truths for Living with Purpose, Strength, and Integrity is a call to awaken the soul of manhood. It's not just a book—it's a companion for the road ahead. It speaks to the man who feels lost in the noise, the one who's tired of pretending, and the one who knows there's more to life than survival. Whether you're stepping into adulthood, navigating the complexities of marriage, or carrying the weight of fatherhood, this book meets you with grace and grit. It's a guide to becoming—not just better, but whole.

Each chapter is crafted to uncover the layers of identity that often go unexplored. You'll wrestle with the question: Who am I? Beyond the roles you play, beyond the expectations placed on you, lies a deeper truth—one rooted in divine design. You'll discover the sacredness of brotherhood, where loyalty and vulnerability coexist. You'll explore friendshiphood, where iron sharpens iron. You'll embrace fatherhood, not as a burden, but as a legacy. You'll learn the humility of sonhood and the devotion of husbandhood. These aren't just titles—they're reflections of who you were created to be.

You'll confront the real struggles men face. Insecurity that whispers you're not enough. Social awkwardness that keeps you isolated. The ache for connection that's often buried beneath pride. You'll learn how to set boundaries that protect without pushing people away. You'll navigate sex and desire with integrity, confronting the temptations of infidelity and onanism with honesty and grace. These chapters don't condemn—they heal. They offer truth that liberates and wisdom that restores.

Discipline and self-care are reframed as lifelines, not luxuries. You'll learn how to steward your body, renew your mind, and nourish your spirit. You'll explore godly character—not as a checklist, but as a way of life. You'll be handed a blueprint for intentional living, a guide to understanding your strengths and weaknesses, and a framework for stepping into your rightful position—not as a tyrant, but as a servant-leader.

You'll meet the hero within—the protector, the provider, the man who rises when others retreat. And you'll meet the champion—the one who fights not for applause, but for legacy. You'll learn to live from the heart, where authenticity resides, rather than the head, where fear and calculation often dominate. You'll embrace the math of manhood: what to add (wisdom, courage, grace), what to subtract (shame, addiction, comparison), what to divide (time, energy, responsibility), and what to multiply (love, truth, impact).

You'll be reminded that men are called to serve an Unrivalled God—the one true source of strength. In Him, you'll find identity, integrity, initiative, and purpose. Like Moses, who found courage in God's presence. Like Caleb, who stood firm when others doubted. Like Paul, who turned his past into a mission. You'll be called to stand in that strength—not just for yourself, but for your family, your workplace, and your community.

You'll explore the Unrivalled Mission—empowering each other to live intentionally, challenging men to be active participants in the life of the church, and inspiring bold, authentic witness. You'll see it in men like Nehemiah, who rebuilt with purpose, and Philip, who shared the gospel on the road. You'll be reminded that mission isn't reserved for the pulpit—it's lived in everyday obedience.

And you'll be invited into your Unrivalled Calling—You'll learn to overcome fear, comparison, and past failures. You'll see yourself in Gideon, who doubted but obeyed. In Peter, who failed but was restored. In Jeremiah, who felt inadequate but was chosen. Faith in Christ frees you to step fully into God's purpose. You'll be challenged to show up— not just physically, but spiritually. To engage, to lead, to serve.

This book is not about perfection. It's about becoming. It's about peeling back the layers, facing the truth, and stepping into the fullness of who you are. It's about learning to live with purpose, strength, and integrity—not just for yourself, but for those who follow you. Welcome to the journey. You're not alone. And you're not too late.

Chapter One

WHO YOU ARE AS A MAN?

I used to think being a man meant being tough. Not just physically, but emotionally. I thought it meant never crying, never showing weakness, never asking for help. I believed that manhood was something you earned through grit and silence, through enduring pain without complaint. That's what I saw growing up. My father was a quiet man, strong in the way that made you feel safe but distant in the way that made you wonder if he ever felt anything deeply. He worked hard, came home tired, and rarely spoke about what was going on inside him. I admired him, but I also feared becoming him.

As I got older, I started to realize that manhood wasn't what I thought it was. It wasn't about hiding. It wasn't about pretending. It wasn't about being invincible. It was something deeper, something quieter, something harder to define. I began to ask myself: Who am I as a man? What does it mean to carry this identity in a world that keeps changing its definition?

Manhood, I've learned, isn't a destination. It's not a badge you earn or a role you perform. It's a journey—a lifelong process of becoming. It's about learning to live with integrity, to love with courage, to lead with humility, and to stand with conviction. It's not about being perfect. It's about being honest.

Who you are as a man, from God's perspective, is not defined by the world's standards of success, strength, or status. It is rooted in something far deeper—your identity as His creation, His son, and His reflection. From the very beginning, God formed man with intention and care. Genesis 1:27 tells us that "God created man in His own image." That means you carry the imprint of the divine. You were made to reflect God's character—His creativity, His justice, His compassion, and His strength.

God sees you not just as a worker or a provider, but as a steward of His love and truth. You are called to lead with humility, to protect with gentleness, and to serve with courage. In Ephesians 5:25, Paul writes, "Husbands, love your wives, just as Christ loved the church and gave Himself up for her." This isn't just about marriage—it's about the kind of sacrificial love God calls every man to embody. You are meant to be a safe place for others, someone who builds rather than breaks, who lifts rather than burdens.

But God also knows your limitations. He doesn't expect perfection—He desires relationship. Micah 6:8 says, "He has shown you, O man, what is good; and what does the Lord require of you but to do justice, to love mercy, and to walk humbly with your God?" Humility is not weakness. It is the posture of a man who knows he needs grace. It's the soil where wisdom grows.

You are also called to courage. Not the kind that puffs up the chest, but the kind that stands firm in truth when it's unpopular, that chooses integrity over comfort. First Corinthians 16:13–14 says, "Be watchful, stand firm in the faith, act like men, be strong. Let all that you do be done in love." God's vision of manhood is not passive—it's active, bold, and rooted in love.

Above all, you are loved. Deeply. Unconditionally. You are not defined by your failures or your past. Through Christ, you are redeemed and made new. Second Corinthians 5:17 reminds us, "If anyone is in Christ, he is a new creation. The old has passed away; behold, the new has come." You are not striving for worth—you already have it. You are a son of God, cherished and chosen.

Being a man of God is not a destination—it's a journey. It's a daily walk of becoming more like Christ, of leaning into grace, and of living with purpose. You are not alone in that journey. God walks with you, shaping you, strengthening you, and calling you forward.

You were created in the image of God. That truth alone carries immense weight. Genesis 1:26–27 tells us that God made man in His likeness, giving him dominion over creation. This isn't about control—it's about stewardship. You were designed to cultivate, to care, to lead with wisdom and compassion. Being made in God's image means you carry His fingerprints: the capacity to create, to reason, to love, and to lead. It means your life has inherent dignity and worth, regardless of what the world says.

God also gave you a purpose. You're not here by accident. Jeremiah 29:11 reminds us, "For I know the plans I have for you," declares the Lord, "plans to prosper you and not to harm you, plans to give you hope and a future." Your purpose isn't just about career or success—it's about living a life that reflects God's heart. Colossians 3:23 encourages you to "work heartily, as for the Lord and not for men." Whether you're building a business, raising a family, or serving your community, your work matters when it's done with integrity and love.

Strength is a key part of biblical manhood, but it's not just physical. It's emotional, spiritual, and moral. Joshua 1:9 says, "Be strong and courageous. Do not be afraid; do not be discouraged, for the Lord your God will be with you wherever you go." Strength in God's eyes is about standing firm in truth, even when it's unpopular. It's about protecting those who are vulnerable, speaking up for what's right, and persevering through trials with faith.

Leadership is another calling placed on men, but it's not about dominance—it's about service. Ephesians 5:23 describes the husband as the head of the wife, as Christ is the head of the church. But Christ's leadership was marked by sacrifice, humility, and love. He washed feet. He laid down His life. That's the model of leadership God calls men to follow. It's about guiding with grace, listening with empathy, and making decisions that honour God and bless others.

Humility is the foundation of all godly character. Micah 6:8 tells us that what God requires is "to do justice, to love mercy, and to walk humbly with your God." A humble man knows he doesn't have all the answers. He's teachable, repentant, and aware of his need for grace. David, though a mighty king and warrior, was called "a man after God's own heart" because he was quick to repent, to worship, and to seek God's will.

Love is the heartbeat of biblical manhood. First Corinthians 16:13–14 says, "Be watchful, stand firm in the faith, act like men, be strong. Let all that you do be done in love." True masculinity is not cold or detached—it's deeply relational. It's about loving your family, your friends, your community, and even your enemies with the kind of love that Jesus showed. That love is patient, kind, selfless, and enduring.

Finally, your identity as a man is rooted in redemption. You are not defined by your past, your failures, or your weaknesses. Through Christ, you are made new. Second Corinthians 5:17 declares, "If anyone is in Christ, he is a new creation. The old has passed away; behold, the new has come." You are a son of God, chosen, forgiven, and empowered to live a life of purpose and impact.

Being a man of God is not about perfection—it's about pursuit. It's about daily surrender, daily growth, and daily reflection of Christ. Whether you're young or old, single or married, thriving or struggling, God sees you. He knows you. And He calls you to rise—not in pride, but in purpose. To be the man He created you to be.

I remember one night, sitting alone in my parent's home after a breakup that shook me more than I expected. I was only 17 years old. I had loved her deeply, but I hadn't known how to show it. I had tried to be strong, to be the man I thought she needed—decisive, composed, always in control. But in doing so, I had shut her out. I had hidden my fears, my doubts, my tenderness. And when she left saying, "I allowed someone else in my life," I realized I had been performing manhood, not living it.

That night, I cried. Not the kind of tears that come quietly, but the kind that break you open. And in that moment, something shifted. I felt more like a man than I ever had before. Not because I was broken, but because I was real. I wasn't hiding anymore. I wasn't pretending. I was just me—flawed, vulnerable, and still worthy and that's when I did a brain reset and migrated to Canada.

Manhood, I've come to believe, is about presence. It's about showing up—for yourself, for others, for the life you're meant to live. It's about asking hard questions and sitting with uncomfortable answers. It's about choosing responsibility over escape, truth over convenience, love over fear.

It's also about knowing your story. Every man carries a story—of where he came from, what shaped him, what wounded him, and what he dreams of. And until you know your story, you'll keep repeating it. You'll keep chasing approval, avoiding pain, and trying to prove something that doesn't need proving. But when you begin to own your story, you begin to live with freedom. You stop reacting and start responding. You stop performing and start becoming.

I've had moments where I felt like I didn't measure up. Times when I lost a job, failed in parenting, in my marriage with Kathleen not being there enough disappointed people I cared about. In those moments, I questioned my worth. I wondered if I was enough. But slowly, I began to understand that manhood isn't about never falling—it's about how you rise. It's about how you learn, how you grow, how you keep showing up even when it's hard.

Being a man means embracing paradox. It means being strong and tender, bold and humble, driven and patient. It means knowing when to speak and when to listen, when to fight and when to forgive. It means carrying weight without being crushed by it, and asking for help without shame.

I've learned that the men I admire most aren't the ones who have it all together. They're the ones who are honest about their struggles, who live with purpose, who love deeply and lead quietly. They're the ones who make you feel seen, who challenge you to grow, who remind you that you're not alone.

Manhood is not a mask. It's not a role. It's a way of being. It's about becoming the kind of man who makes the world better—not by force, but by presence. The kind of man who builds, who heals, who protects, who serves.

One of the most defining moments in my journey as a man came when I became a father in 1991. Holding my newborn daughter Karleen in my arms, I felt a weight I had never known before. It wasn't fear—it was responsibility. Suddenly, I wasn't just living for myself. I was shaping someone else's world. Every word I spoke, every choice I made, every moment I showed up—or didn't—would leave a mark. That realization didn't make me feel powerful. It made me feel humble.

Fatherhood taught me that manhood isn't about control—it's about presence. It's about being there, even when you're tired, even when you're unsure, even when you feel like you're failing. It's about showing up with your whole heart, not just your hands. I've made mistakes as a father. I've lost my temper, missed important moments, said things I wish I could take back. But I've also learned to apologize, to listen, to grow. And in doing so, I've become more of a man—not less.

There's a quiet strength in admitting you don't have all the answers. I used to think I had to be the rock—unshakable, unbreakable. But I've learned that being a rock doesn't mean being rigid. It means being steady. It means being dependable. It means being someone others can lean on, not someone who refuses to bend.

I've had seasons in my life where I felt lost. Times when I didn't know what I was working toward, when my days felt like a blur of obligations and distractions. I chased success, thinking it would give me clarity. I chased relationships, hoping they would give me identity. I chased approval, believing it would give me worth. But none of those things filled the ache inside me. Because manhood isn't found in what you chase—it's found in what you choose.

I had to choose to slow down. To listen to the quiet voice inside me that asked, "What kind of man do you want to be?" Not what kind of job I wanted, or what kind of house I dreamed of, or what kind of reputation I hoped to build. But what kind of man. That question changed everything.

I started to pay attention to the men around me—the ones who seemed grounded, generous, wise. They weren't flashy. They weren't loud. They didn't need to be. They carried themselves with a kind of peace that came from knowing who they were. They didn't need to prove anything. They just lived with purpose.

One of those men was my father. He was a quiet man, but when he spoke, people listened. He didn't talk about success—he talked about service. He didn't boast about what he had—he gave freely. He didn't demand respect—he earned it. Watching him, I realized that manhood isn't about being the center of attention. It's about being the center of stability.

Every man has a moment when he realizes that strength isn't enough. That being capable, competent, and confident can only take you so far. At some point, you have to ask yourself: Am I living with integrity? Am I living with love? Am I living with courage?

Courage, I've found, isn't about facing danger. It's about facing yourself. It's about looking in the mirror and being honest about what you see. It's about confronting your fears, your failures, your flaws—and choosing to grow. That kind of courage doesn't roar. It whispers. It says, "Keep going."

Manhood isn't about being flawless. It's about being faithful—to your values, to your growth, to the people who depend on you. It's about learning from your mistakes, not being defined by them. It's about becoming better, not bitter.

I've also learned that manhood is deeply relational. You can't become a man in isolation. You need other men—brothers, mentors, friends—who challenge you, support you, and call you higher. I've had men in my life who saw something in me I couldn't see in myself. They believed in me when I didn't. They spoke truth when I needed it. They reminded me that I wasn't alone.

And I've tried to be that man for others. To show up. To listen. To speak life. To be a safe place. Because manhood isn't just about who you are—it's about how you impact others. It's about legacy.

Legacy isn't built in grand gestures. It's built-in everyday choices. In how you treat your spouse. In how you raise your children. In how you handle conflict. In how you show up when it's inconvenient. In how you live when no one's watching.

I want my legacy to be love. Not the soft kind that avoids hard truths, but the fierce kind that fights for what matters. I want to be remembered as a man who lived with integrity, who led with humility, who loved with courage. I want my life to echo in the lives of others—not because I was perfect, but because I was present.

So, if you're reading this and wondering who you are as a man, let me say this: You are not your failures. You are not your fears. You are not the expectations others have placed on you. You are a work in progress. You are a story unfolding. You are a man becoming. And that is enough.

CHAPTER ONE : WHO YOU ARE AS A MAN?

Chapter Two

THE BROTHERHOOD

There's something sacred about the bond between men. Not the kind forged in competition or bravado, but the kind that grows in quiet moments, shared burdens, and unspoken understanding. Brotherhood isn't just about blood—it's about belonging. It's about standing shoulder to shoulder with someone who sees you, knows you, and chooses to walk beside you anyway.

I didn't always understand the value of brotherhood. For a long time, I thought I had to do life alone along with my wife Kathleen and our children. I believed that strength meant self-sufficiency, which asking for help was weakness, that vulnerability was dangerous. I kept my struggles to myself, wore a mask of composure, and convinced myself I was fine. But deep down, I was lonely. Not because I didn't have my family around me—but because I didn't let anyone in.

Then something shifted. I hit a season where everything felt heavy—work, relationships, my own inner battles. I was tired of pretending. One day, I called a friend I hadn't spoken to in months who lives in Germany. Joshua Damm I met in Germany, where he first served as my airport driver and translator—but God had something deeper in store. Over the course of a year, we became prayer partners, meeting faithfully every day at midnight EST and 6am his time. That hour was sacred: filled with prayer, reflection, and conversations about the goodness of God. Through those moments, a true brotherhood was born. It wasn't built on proximity, but on shared faith, trust, and spiritual intimacy. Joshua became more than a voice between languages—he became a brother in Christ, walking beside me in prayer and purpose.

When I called him, I didn't have a script. I just said, "hey bro, bro bro." And as he replied saying the same words, something happened. My day felt refreshed. I felt something I hadn't felt in a while: brotherhood. We chatted, shared about what was going on in each other's life and a joy came into our conversation.

That's what brotherhood does. It gives you a place to be real. A place to be weak. A place to be human.

I've come to believe that every man needs a circle—a few trusted brothers who know the truth about him and still choose to stay. Men who will call him out when he's drifting, lift him up when he's down, and remind him of who he is when he forgets. Not every friendship becomes a brotherhood. But when it does, it's one of the most powerful forces in a man's life.

Brotherhood is built in layers. It starts with shared experiences—working together, laughing together, struggling together. But it deepens through honesty. Through the kind of conversations that go beyond sports and politics and dive into fears, dreams, regrets. I've had late-night talks with men that felt like therapy. We didn't solve anything, but we healed something. Just by being there.

There's a kind of healing that only happens in the presence of another man who's walked through the same fire. I've sat across from men who've lost fathers, battled addiction, faced divorce, questioned their faith. And in those moments, I didn't need to offer wisdom. I just needed to say, "Me too." That's the language of brotherhood—shared pain, shared hope, shared humanity.

Brotherhood is more than shared blood or common interests. In the eyes of God, it is a sacred bond—a reflection of His love, unity, and grace among His people. The Bible speaks of brotherhood not just as a biological connection, but as a spiritual relationship rooted in faith, compassion, and mutual responsibility. It is a call to live in harmony, to lift one another up, and to walk together in truth.

From the earliest pages of Scripture, we see both the beauty and the brokenness of brotherhood. Cain and Abel, the first brothers, remind us of the consequences of jealousy and division. When God asked Cain, "Where is your brother Abel?" (Genesis 4:9), it wasn't just a question—it was a call to accountability. Brotherhood, in God's design, carries the weight of care. We are meant to look out for one another, not turn away.

Yet the Bible doesn't leave us in that brokenness. It paints a richer, redemptive picture of what brotherhood can be. Psalm 133:1 declares, "How good and pleasant it is when brothers live together in unity!" This unity is not passive—it's active. It's forged through forgiveness, humility, and shared purpose. When brothers dwell in peace, it is like "precious oil" and "dew on Mount Hermon"—symbols of blessing, refreshment, and divine favour.

Jesus Himself redefined brotherhood in a radical way. In Mark 3:35, He said, "Whoever does the will of God is my brother and sister and mother." With these words, He expanded the family of God beyond bloodlines. Brotherhood became a spiritual kinship, a community of believers bound together by love and obedience to God. This means that every person who walks in faith is your brother—not just those who share your last name, but those who share your heart for Christ.

Paul's letters echo this truth with tenderness and strength. He often referred to fellow believers as "brothers," emphasizing the depth of connection within the body of Christ. In Romans 12:10, he writes, "Be devoted to one another in love. Honour one another above yourselves." This devotion is not casual—it's committed. It means showing up, speaking truth, and sacrificing for one another. It means choosing to love even when it's hard.

Brotherhood also involves bearing each other's burdens. Galatians 6:2 says, "Carry each other's burdens, and in this way, you will fulfill the law of Christ." This is the kind of love that doesn't flinch at pain. It steps into the mess, offers a shoulder, and says, "You're not alone." In true brotherhood, we don't just celebrate each other's victories—we walk through the valleys together.

And when conflict arises—as it inevitably does—Jesus gives us a path to restoration. In Matthew 18:15–17, He lays out a process for reconciliation, reminding us that brotherhood is worth fighting for. It's not about avoiding hard conversations, but about pursuing peace with courage and grace.

Ultimately, brotherhood is a reflection of God's own nature. The Trinity—Father, Son, and Holy Spirit—exists in perfect unity and relationship. When we live in brotherly love, we mirror that divine harmony. First John 4:21 says, "Anyone who loves God must also love their brother." Our love for one another is not optional—it's evidence of our love for God.

So whether you're walking with lifelong friends, navigating family dynamics, or building bonds within your church, remember this: Brotherhood is holy. It's healing. It's a gift. And when it's rooted in

Christ, it becomes a powerful force for good—a glimpse of heaven on earth.

Brotherhood, in its truest form, is not forged by blood, but by spirit. It's a bond that transcends culture, language, and even war. It's the kind of connection that God Himself honours—a covenant of loyalty, love, and shared purpose.

When I met Tihomir in Croatia, I didn't know that I was about to step into one of the most sacred friendships of my life. I had simply shared Jesus with him. But what followed was something deeper than conversion—it was communion.

We met in Split, a city kissed by the Adriatic Sea and crowned by the quiet majesty of Marijan Mountain. That mountain became our sanctuary. Every morning, before the world stirred, we climbed its paths to pray at 5am. There, in the stillness, we grew—not just in faith, but in brotherhood. We poured out our hearts to God, shared our burdens, and lifted each other up. It was like David and Jonathan all over again. The Bible says, "The soul of Jonathan was knit to the soul of David, and Jonathan loved him as his own soul" (1 Samuel 18:1). That was us. Two men from different worlds, different culture and ethnicity bound together by the Spirit of God.

Tihomir wasn't just a friend. He became family. He loved my wife as if she were his own sister. He protected us fiercely, with a loyalty that made me feel safe and proud. I knew without a shadow of a doubt—he would take a bullet for me. And in many ways, he did. His life was marked by sacrifice, by quiet strength, and by unwavering faith. Even when others mocked our belief, even when the cost of following Jesus was high, he never wavered. He never spoke a negative word. His heart was pure, his love was fierce, and his devotion was unshakable.

That kind of brotherhood is rare. It's not romantic it was bromance. It's not sentimental. It's spiritual. It's the kind of bond that teaches you, stretches you, and makes you better. Proverbs 17:17 says, "A friend loves at all times, and a brother is born for adversity." Tihomir was that brother. Born for adversity. Born to stand beside me when the world turned cold.

When he was killed, a piece of my heart was torn away. I wasn't allowed to attend his funeral. The war and religious tensions made it impossible. People knew he had chosen to follow Jesus, and that choice came with a cost. But even in death, his witness lived on. For 26 years, I carried the ache of that loss. And then, one day, my son and I visited his gravesite. I said my goodbye. I wept. I went down memory lane. And in that moment, something in me began to heal.

Brotherhood like ours doesn't die. It echoes. It shapes you. It reminds you that God places people in your life not just to walk with you, but to carry you when you can't walk alone. Romans 12:10 says, "Be devoted to one another in brotherly love. Honour one another above yourselves." Tihomir lived that verse. He honoured me. He honoured my family. And he honoured the Lord with his life.

So when I speak of brotherhood, I speak of something holy. Something forged in prayer, proven in trial, and sealed in love. It's not about proximity—it's about presence. It's not about shared hobbies— it's about shared hearts. And it's not about how long you walk together, but how deeply you walk while you do.

Tihomir was my Jonathan. And I was his David. And though he's gone, the covenant we shared still lives. In my memory. In my faith. And in the quiet mornings when I still climb the mountain in my heart and whisper, "Thank you, Lord, for my brother."

Brotherhood isn't always easy. It requires effort, vulnerability, forgiveness. Sometimes it means having hard conversations. Sometimes it means showing up when it's inconvenient. Sometimes it means holding space for someone who's hurting, even when you don't have the words. But it's worth it. Because in a world that often tells men to isolate, to compete, to perform—brotherhood offers connection.

I've seen men come alive in the presence of other men who believe in them. I've seen confidence restored, marriages healed, addictions broken—all because someone had the courage to say, "You're not alone." That's the power of brotherhood. It doesn't fix everything, but it makes the journey bearable.

There's a kind of strength that grows in community. Not the loud, aggressive kind—but the quiet, steady kind. The kind that says, "I've got your back." The kind that says, "I see you." The kind that says, "Let's walk this road together."

If you're a man reading this and you feel alone, I want you to know you weren't meant to do life by yourself. You were made for connection. You were made for brotherhood. And it's never too late to find it. Start by reaching out. Start by being honest. Start by showing up.

Because when men stand together, something sacred happens. We become more than individuals—we become a tribe. A force for good. A source of healing. A reflection of what manhood was always meant to be.

Brotherhood is not a luxury. It's a lifeline. And every man deserves it.

There was a time in my life when I thought I had to be the strong one in every room. I didn't want to burden anyone with my problems, didn't want to admit when I was struggling. I thought that was noble. I thought that was manly. But the truth is, it was lonely. I was carrying weight I didn't need to carry alone, and I was missing out on the kind of connection that could have made me stronger—not weaker.

Brotherhood changed that!

It started slowly. A few honest conversations with men I trusted. A few moments where I let my guard down and said, "I don't have it all figured out." And to my surprise, they didn't judge me. They didn't pull away. They learned in. They shared their own stories—their own doubts, their own failures, their own fears. And suddenly, I didn't feel so alone.

There's something powerful about being known. Not just admired or respected, but truly known. Brotherhood offers that. It's the space where you can be fully yourself—messy, imperfect, in progress—and still be accepted. It's where you can laugh until your stomach hurts, cry without shame, and speak truth without fear.

I've had brothers who've walked with me through grieving, betrayal, through career changes, through spiritual crises. They didn't always have the answers, but they had presence. And sometimes, that's all you need. Someone to sit with you in the silence. Someone to remind you that you're not crazy, not broken, not beyond hope.

One of the most meaningful friendships I've ever had started in the most ordinary way. I was speaking at a church in Quebec when I noticed a young man named Jonathan Labrecque holding a Bible with the exact same cover as mine. The only difference—his Bible was in French, and mine in English. He didn't speak a word of English, and I didn't speak a word of French, but that shared detail became our first connection. It was small, almost humorous, but somehow sacred. That Bible cover was the bridge God used to begin something much deeper.

Over time, Jonathan began learning English, and our conversations slowly grew from simple greetings to heartfelt exchanges. We started talking about our marriages, our insecurities, our dreams, and the things that weighed on our hearts. What began as a casual encounter turned into a spiritual bond. Before I knew it, he had become a brother—not because we shared DNA, but because we shared life. We shared faith. We shared vulnerability.

Jonathan is a worship leader, and his love for the Lord is evident in everything he does. His wife and son are worshippers too, and seeing their family live out their faith together made brotherhood with him feel natural and deeply encouraging. There was no pretense in our friendship—just honesty, prayer, and mutual respect. We didn't need perfect language to understand each other. The Spirit translated what words couldn't.

Brotherhood with Jonathan reminded me that God often uses the simplest things—a Bible cover, a shared prayer, a quiet moment—to build something eternal. Our friendship is a testimony that when hearts are open, and Christ is at the center, language barriers fade, and true connection begins.

Brotherhood isn't about perfection. It's about commitment. It's about showing up, again and again, even when it's inconvenient. It's about choosing to stay when things get messy. It's about being the kind of man who doesn't run when things get hard.

When I met Jachin Mullen, the first thing he said was, "You have to meet my tribe." At the time, I wasn't sure what he meant, but it quickly became clear—he was thinking of connecting me to a group of his friends who were part of his brotherhood. Jachin is another David in my life, a man whose presence has reminded me that character and personality are keys that open doors into meaningful relationships. He has inspired me in more ways than he probably realizes and came into my life at exactly the right time.

Jachin didn't just introduce me to his brothers in the Lord; he opened his heart. He chose transparency, and through that, we've been able to share deeply. There's something powerful about a man who doesn't just speak about connection but lives it. His example of brotherhood is rare and refreshing. We need more Jachins in our lives—men who are willing to be real, to reach out, and to walk alongside others with sincerity and strength. True brotherhood isn't built on surface-level talk;

it's built on shared truth, mutual respect, and the kind of love that reflects something eternal.

I've learned that brotherhood requires vulnerability. And vulnerability requires courage. It's not easy to say, "I'm hurting," or "I'm scared," or "I need help." But every time I've had the courage to speak those words, I've found connection. I've found healing. I've found strength.

There's a myth that men are supposed to be lone wolves. That we're supposed to figure things out on our own, carry our burdens in silence, and never let anyone see us sweat. But that myth is killing us. It's isolating us. It's robbing us of the very thing we need most: each other.

I've seen what happens when men choose brotherhood. I've seen addictions lose their grip. I've seen marriages restored. I've seen purpose reignited. Not because someone swooped in with all the answers, but because someone stayed. Someone listened. Someone believed.

Brotherhood is a mirror. It shows you who you are, and who you're becoming. It challenges you to grow, to rise, to become the man you were meant to be. It doesn't let you settle. It doesn't let you hide. It calls you out, and it calls you up.

I've had brothers who've told me hard truths—truths I didn't want to hear, but needed to. They've said, "You're drifting," or "You're not being honest," or "You're better than this." And because I knew they loved me, I listened. I changed. I grew.

That's the beauty of brotherhood. It's not just about comfort—it's about transformation.

And it's not just about receiving—it's about giving. I've had the privilege of being that brother for others. Of sitting with a friend who just lost his job, or just buried his father, or just found out his marriage was falling apart. I didn't have magic words. But I had presence. I had empathy. I had love.

Sometimes, the most powerful thing you can say is, "I'm here."

Brotherhood also brings joy. It's not all heavy conversations and deep reflections. It's road trips and inside jokes and backyard barbecues. It's watching the game together, teasing each other, celebrating wins. It's the kind of laughter that reminds your life is still good, even when it's hard.

I've found that the older I get, the more I value these relationships. Not just acquaintances, but true brothers. Men who know my story, who know my heart, who know my flaws—and still choose me. That kind of connection is rare. And when you find it, you hold onto it.

If you're reading this and you don't have that kind of brotherhood, I want to encourage you: it's possible. It starts with one honest conversation. One moment of courage. One step toward connection. You don't have to wait for someone else to initiate. You can be the one who reaches out. You can be the one who says, "Let's talk," or "I've been thinking about you," or "I'm here."

Because every man needs a brother. And every man can be one.

Brotherhood is a gift. It's a refuge. It's a fire that refines and a shelter that protects. It's where we become more than we could ever be alone.

And it's one of the things every man should know.

CHAPTER TWO : THE BROTHERHOOD

Chapter Three

FRIENDSHIPHOOD

There's a kind of friendship that goes beyond casual connection. It's not just about shared interests or proximity—it's about shared life. I call it friendshiphood. It's the space where trust is built, where laughter is healing, and where silence is safe. It's where men find a kind of companionship that doesn't need to be loud to be strong.

I've had friends come and go over the years. Some drifted away with time, others faded after seasons changed. But a few stayed. A few dug in. A few became more than friends—they became anchors. And looking back, I realize that those friendships didn't just happen. They were built. Slowly. Intentionally. Sometimes painfully. It's the kind of bond that doesn't require performance. You don't have to be impressive. You just must be present.

I've learned that real friendship between men is rare—not because we don't want it, but because we're not always taught how to build it. We're taught to compete, to compare, to keep things light. We joke, we tease, we talk about sports and work and weather. But underneath all that, there's a hunger. A longing to be known. To be understood. To be accepted.

I've had moments where I wanted to open up to a friend but didn't know how. I didn't want to be a burden. I didn't want to seem weak. But every time I've taken that risk—every time I've said, "I'm struggling," or "I'm scared," or "I need someone to talk to"—I've found connection. Not always perfectly. Not always easily. But enough to remind me that I'm not alone.

When we talk about relationships—especially among men—it's important to recognize the layers of connection that exist. Not every person we meet is meant to become a brother, but every brother once started as a stranger. There's a natural progression in human connection that moves from acquaintance, to friendship, and in rare cases, to brotherhood. Each stage carries its own depth, and understanding the difference helps us appreciate the value of those who walk closely with us.

Acquaintances are the people we meet in passing. They might be coworkers, neighbours, or someone we've shared a meal or a moment with while travelling. There's politeness, maybe even familiarity, but not much vulnerability. Acquaintances are important—they're the doorway to deeper relationships—but they remain on the surface. You know their name, maybe a few facts about their life, but you don't share your heart with them.

Friendshiphood is the next layer. Friends are those you choose to spend time with. You laugh together, share stories, and build trust through shared experiences. There's emotional connection, and often a sense of mutual support. Friends are the ones you call when something good happens—or when life gets hard. But friendship, while meaningful, can still be conditional. It may depend on proximity, shared interests, or seasons of life. Some friendships fade over time, and that's okay. They serve a purpose, and they leave an imprint.

Brotherhood, though, is something deeper. It's forged through loyalty, sacrifice, and spiritual alignment. Brotherhood isn't just about enjoying each other's company—it's about standing in the gap for one another. It's about showing up when it's inconvenient, praying when words fail, and loving without conditions. A brother is someone who knows your flaws and still chooses to stay. He's someone who carries your burdens as if they were his own. Brotherhood is rare because it requires vulnerability, consistency, and a shared commitment to something greater than yourselves.

In my own life, I've met incredible men across the world—in Peru, Brazil, Argentina, the Philippines, Holland, Croatia, Germany, Spain, the United States and Canada. Many of them started as acquaintances. Some became friends. We shared meals, laughter, and good company. But only a few crossed into the sacred space of brotherhood. That transition doesn't happen by accident. It happens when hearts connect, when trust is built, and when faith is shared.

The goal isn't to force every relationship into brotherhood. It's to recognize the potential in each connection. To be open to the journey. Because sometimes, the man you meet in passing—the one you barely know—might one day become the person who walks with you through your deepest valleys. And when that happens, you'll know this is more than friendship. This is brotherhood.

Friendshiphood is built on honesty. Not just about the good stuff, but about the hard stuff. It's built on showing up, even when it's inconvenient. It's built on forgiveness because we all mess up. It's built on grace because we all fall short.

I've had friends who've challenged me. Who've called me out when I was drifting. Who've asked hard questions when I was avoiding truth.

And I've had to do the same. That's part of the deal. Real friendship isn't just about comfort—it's about growth. It's about helping each other become better men.

There was a season in my life when I was deeply discouraged. Work was overwhelming, my marriage was strained, and I felt like I was failing in every direction. I didn't want to talk about it. I didn't want to admit it. But one day, a friend showed up with two cups of coffee and said, "I don't know what's going on, but I'm not leaving until we talk." We sat for hours. I cried. He listened. And by the end of the night, I felt lighter. Not because anything had changed—but because someone had carried the weight with me.

That's what friendshiphood does. It shares the load. It doesn't fix everything, but it makes the journey bearable.

I've also learned that friendshiphood requires intentionality. Life gets busy. Responsibilities pile up. And if we're not careful, our friendships become background noise. But the best ones—the ones that last—are the ones we fight for. The ones we prioritize. The ones we protect.

Sometimes that means sending a text just to check in. Sometimes it means planning a weekend away. Sometimes it means making space for a phone call, even when you're tired. It doesn't have to be grand—it just has to be consistent.

I've found that the older I get, the more I value these relationships. Not just for the fun, but for the depth. For the history. For the shared memories and the shared scars. There's something sacred about walking through life with someone who's seen you at your worst and still chooses you.

Friendshiphood also teaches you how to be a better man. It teaches you patience, empathy, humility. It teaches you to listen, to forgive, to show up. It reminds you that you're not the center of the universe—and that's a good thing.

If you're reading this and you feel disconnected, I want you to know it's never too late to build friendshiphood. It starts with one honest conversation. One act of courage. One moment of reaching out, its killing the pride and making an effort to connect.

The Bible offers a rich and heartfelt view of male friendshiphood, portraying it as a source of strength, loyalty, and spiritual growth. Friendship among men is not just about companionship—it's about walking together through life's challenges, encouraging one another in faith, and standing firm in truth. Scripture gives us several powerful examples that show how deep and transformative these relationships can be.

One of the most well-known friendships in the Bible is between David and Jonathan who were in the brotherhood circle of each other, loyal and honourable. Their bond went far beyond casual connection. The Bible says that Jonathan's soul was knit to David's, and he loved him as his own soul. Despite Jonathan being the son of King Saul—David's rival—he chose to protect and support David, even at great personal cost. Their friendship was marked by covenant, sacrifice, and unwavering loyalty. It's a model of brotherhood that shows how spiritual alignment and mutual respect can create a bond stronger than blood.

Another example is the relationship between Moses and Aaron. Though they were brothers by birth, their friendshiphood in leading Israel was rooted in trust and shared calling. Aaron stood beside Moses during some of the most difficult moments of his leadership, speaking on his behalf and supporting him when he felt inadequate. Their relationship reminds us that male friendship can be a source of courage and stability, especially when facing overwhelming responsibility.

Paul and Timothy also demonstrate a powerful friendshiphood rooted in mentorship and spiritual growth. Paul referred to Timothy as his beloved son in the faith, and their relationship was built on mutual encouragement and shared mission. Paul poured into Timothy's life, guiding him, affirming him, and trusting him with leadership. This kind of friendship shows how older and younger men can walk together, each strengthening the other.

Jesus Himself modeled male friendship with His disciples. Though He was their teacher and Lord, He called them friends. He lived with them, shared meals, prayed with them, and ultimately laid down His life for them. In John's Gospel, Jesus says, "Greater love has no one than this, that someone lay down his life for his friends." This statement captures the heart of biblical friendshiphood—sacrificial love, rooted in commitment and grace.

The book of Proverbs also offers timeless wisdom about male friendship. It teaches that a friend loves at all times, and a brother is born for adversity. It warns against superficial relationships and celebrates those who stick closer than a brother. These verses remind us that true friendship is not about convenience—it's about presence, especially in times of hardship.

In all these examples, the Bible affirms that male friendship is a gift from God. It's a place where men can be vulnerable, challenged, and uplifted. It's not just about shared interests—it's about shared hearts, shared faith, and shared purpose. Whether through laughter, prayer, or walking through trials, biblical friendship among men is a sacred bond that reflects the love and loyalty of God Himself.

Chapter Four

FATHERHOOD

I remember the moment I became a father. Not the technical moment, not the delivery room where I cut the umbilical cord or the first cry, but the moment it hit me—this tiny human was mine. Not as a possession, but as a responsibility. A gift. A calling. I looked down at my daughter Karleen, wrapped in a blanket, eyes barely open, and I felt something shift inside me. It wasn't fear, though there was plenty of that. It was reverence. A quiet awe. A sense that life had just changed forever.

Fatherhood is not something you master. It's something you grow into. Slowly. Clumsily. Sometimes painfully. It's a journey of learning to love in ways you didn't know you could, and to sacrifice in ways you didn't know you'd have to.

I wasn't ready. I don't think any man truly is. You can read the books, watch the videos, ask the questions—but nothing prepares you for the moment your child looks at you and sees safety. Sees home. Sees the man who will shape their world.

That kind of weight doesn't crush you—it carves you.

I've made mistakes as a father of seven children. More than I'd like to admit. I've lost my patience, said things I regret, missed moments I can't get back. But I've also learned to apologize. To listen. To grow. And in doing so, I've taught my children something more valuable than perfection—I've taught them humility.

The Bible paints a beautiful and reverent picture of fatherhood—one that goes far beyond provision and discipline. It's a calling to nurture, guide, bless, and reflect the heart of God to the next generation. Raising seven children—six daughters and one son—is not just a responsibility, but a divine privilege. And walking with them into adulthood, alongside my wife Kathleen, is a testimony to the enduring joy and sacred weight of fatherhood.

Scripture reminds us that children are not burdens—they are blessings. *"Behold, children are a heritage from the Lord, the fruit of the womb a reward"* (Psalm 127:3). Each child is a gift, entrusted to you for a season, to be shaped, loved, and launched into their own calling. Watching your children marry, mature, and become their own people is a reward that few things in life can match. It's in those moments—weddings, milestones, quiet conversations—that the seeds you planted as a father begin to bloom.

Proverbs 22:6 offers timeless wisdom: *"Train up a child in the way he should go; even when he is old he will not depart from it."* This verse speaks to the long arc of parenting. It's not just about the early years—it's about consistency, presence, and spiritual investment that lasts a lifetime. And when you see your adult children walking in faith, building families of their own, and carrying forward the values you instilled, it's a reflection of God's faithfulness through your fatherhood.

Being a grandfather adds another layer of richness. It's not just an extension of parenting—it's a new chapter of influence, gentleness, and legacy. Proverbs 17:6 says, *"Children's children are a crown to the aged, and parents are the pride of their children."* Grandfatherhood allows you to enjoy the fruit of your labor with a softer touch. You become a storyteller, a spiritual anchor, and a source of wisdom for the next generation.

Deuteronomy 6:6–7 also speaks to the rhythm of fatherhood: *"These commandments that I give you today are to be on your hearts. Impress them on your children. Talk about them when you sit at home and when you walk along the road, when you lie down and when you get up."* This passage reminds us that fatherhood is not just about big moments—it's about daily presence. It's about weaving faith into the fabric of everyday life.

My journey with Kathleen—raising seven children, walking through each stage of development, and now embracing the joy of grandfatherhood—is a living testimony of God's design for family. It's a reminder that fatherhood is not just a role—it's a legacy. And every hug, prayer, and word of encouragement you've offered has echoed into the lives of your children and grandchildren.

If you ever feel the weight of the years, remember you've built something eternal. And the joy of fatherhood, especially when shared with a faithful spouse, is one of the greatest blessings this life can offer.

Fatherhood isn't about being flawless. It's about being faithful. It's about showing up, day after day, even when you're tired, even when you're unsure, even when you feel like you're failing. It's about being present—not just physically, but emotionally. It's about being the kind of man your children can trust, not because you always get it right, but because you never walk away.

I've learned that children don't need a hero. They need a father. Someone who listens. Someone who leads. Someone who loves without condition. They need your time more than your money. Your attention more than your advice. Your presence more than your perfection.

There was a night when my daughter Kanesha couldn't sleep. She was scared—of the dark, of the shadows, of something she couldn't name. I sat beside her bed, holding her hand, whispering that she was safe. And in that moment, I realized something: my voice had power. Not because it was loud, but because it was hers. Because it was familiar. Because it was steady.

That's what fatherhood is. It's being the steady voice in the chaos. The calm in the storm. The anchor in the drift.

It's also being the mirror. Your children will watch you more than they'll listen to you. They'll learn how to treat others by how you treat their mother. They'll learn how to handle anger by how you handle yours. They'll learn what love looks like by how you love them—and how you love yourself.

That's a sobering thought. But it's also a beautiful one. Because it means every moment matters. Every word, every gesture, every choice—it all adds up. It all shapes the story they'll carry into adulthood.

I've had to confront parts of myself I didn't want to face because of fatherhood. My impatience. My pride. My fear. But in doing so, I've become a better man. Not just for them—but for me. Fatherhood doesn't just change your schedule. It changes your soul.

It teaches you to slow down. To pay attention. To find joy in the ordinary. A walk to the park. A messy breakfast. A bedtime story. These moments don't seem significant—but they are. They're the threads that weave a childhood. And one day, they'll be the memories your children hold onto when they're grown.

I've also learned that fatherhood is not just about giving—it's about receiving. My children have taught me more about grace, wonder, and unconditional love than any book ever could. They've shown me what it means to forgive quickly, to laugh freely, to love fully. They've reminded me that life is not about control—it's about connection.

There's a sacredness to being a father. A quiet holiness. You are shaping a soul. You are guiding a heart. You are building a legacy.

And you won't always see the fruit right away. Sometimes, it feels like you're planting seeds in dry soil. But keep planting. Keep watering. Keep showing up. Because one day, those seeds will bloom. And you'll see the person your child has become—and know that you played a part.

If you're a father reading this, I want to say: you matter. More than you know. Your presence matters. Your words matter. Your love matters. You don't have to be perfect. You just must be present.

And if you're not a father yet, or never will be, know this: the spirit of fatherhood is not limited to biology. It's about mentorship. It's about protection. It's about love. Every man has the ability to father—to nurture, to guide, to build.

Fatherhood is not a role. It's a calling. And it's one of the things every man should know.

CHAPTER FOUR : FATHERHOOD

Chapter Five

SONHOOD

I've spent a lot of time thinking about what it means to be a son. Not just in the literal sense, but in the deeper, more enduring way. Sonhood isn't just about being born into a family—it's about being shaped by it. It's about carrying stories, absorbing lessons, wrestling with expectations, and learning how to honour what came before you while becoming who you're meant to be.

For me, sonhood began with watching my father. He was a man of few words, but his actions spoke volumes. I watched how he treated people, how he handled pressure, how he carried responsibility. I watched him fix things around the house, pay bills, drive in silence after long days. I didn't always understand him, and sometimes I resented the distance between us. But I knew he loved me. Not in the loud, expressive way—but in the steady, reliable way. He showed up. He stayed. He sacrificed.

As a son, I learned early on that love doesn't always look the way you expect it to. Sometimes it's quiet. Sometimes it's flawed. Sometimes it's buried beneath layers of pain and pride. But it's there. And part of sonhood is learning how to see it, receive it, and eventually—return it.

I've had moments where I felt like I disappointed my parents. Times when I made choices they didn't understand, walked paths they wouldn't have chosen. And I've carried that weight—the weight of wanting to make them proud, wanting to live up to something I couldn't quite name. That's part of sonhood too. The tension between independence and belonging. The desire to be your own man, while still honouring the people who raised you.

There was a season in my life when I pulled away from my family. I needed space. I needed to figure out who I was outside of their expectations. I stopped calling as often, stopped visiting, stopped sharing. And for a while, I felt free. But then something shifted. I missed them. Not just their presence, but their history. Their wisdom. Their grounding. I realized that being a son doesn't mean losing yourself—it means knowing where you come from.

Being a son means learning how to forgive. Your parents aren't perfect. They've made mistakes. They've said things they shouldn't have; done things they regret. But they've also loved you in the best way they knew how. And part of growing up is learning how to hold both truths—the pain and the love—and choosing to heal.

It also means learning how to honour. Not blindly, not out of obligation, but out of gratitude. I've come to see my parents not just as authority figures, but as people. People with their own stories, their own wounds, their own dreams. And the more I understand them, the more I understand myself.

Sonhood is also about legacy. You carry more than your name—you carry your family's history. Their values. Their sacrifices. Their hopes. And whether you realize it or not, you're part of a story that began long before you were born. You're a continuation of something sacred. And you get to decide what you'll carry forward—and what you'll leave behind.

I've thought a lot about what kind of son I want to be. Not just to my parents, but to the world. To the generations before me. To the mentors who've poured into me. To the men who've walked ahead and paved the way. I want to be a son who listens. Who learns. Who honours. Who grows.

And I want to be a son who becomes a father—not just biologically, but spiritually. I want to take what I've received and pass it on. I want to build on the foundation I've been given. I want to live in a way that makes my parents proud—not because I followed their path, but because I walked mine with integrity.

One of the clearest expressions of sonhood is found in John 1:12, which says, "Yet to all who did receive him, to those who believed in his name, he gave the right to become children of God." This verse highlights that sonhood is not just a natural status—it is a spiritual gift. Through faith in Jesus Christ, we are adopted into God's family, not as distant followers but as sons with full access to the Father's heart. Romans 8:15 expands on this, saying, "You have received the Spirit of adoption as sons, by whom we cry, 'Abba! Father!'" That cry of "Abba" reflects intimacy, trust, and deep relational connection.

The Bible also offers many stories that illustrate the dynamics of father-son relationships. Abraham and Isaac's story in Genesis 22 is a powerful example of trust and obedience. Isaac's willingness to follow his father, even in the face of sacrifice, and Abraham's faith in God's provision, show a bond built on spiritual trust.

Another example is Jacob and Joseph. Though Jacob favoured Joseph, which led to family tension, their relationship was ultimately restored through forgiveness and grace. Joseph's journey from betrayal to reconciliation with his father is a testament to the resilience of sonhood.

David and Solomon also provide insight into the father-son dynamic. David, despite his flaws, gave Solomon wise counsel before his death, urging him to walk faithfully with God. Solomon's early reign reflected that wisdom, though his later choices showed how sonhood must be continually nurtured. These stories remind us that fatherhood is not just about instruction—it's about presence, consistency, and spiritual investment.

The Bible also warns of the consequences when fatherhood is absent or broken. Eli, the priest, failed to discipline his sons, Hophni and Phinehas, who acted corruptly in their priestly roles. Their behaviour led to judgment on Eli's household, showing that neglecting the role of a father can have serious spiritual and relational consequences.

David's relationship with Absalom is another tragic example. Absalom's rebellion and eventual death left David heartbroken, crying out, "O my son Absalom! My son, my son Absalom! Would I had died instead of you!" This grief reflects the pain of unresolved conflict and missed opportunities for reconciliation.

Sonhood, when nurtured with love, discipline, and spiritual guidance, becomes a place of flourishing. Proverbs 3:11–12 says, "My son, do not despise the Lord's discipline… for the Lord disciplines those he loves, as a father the son in whom he delights." Discipline, when rooted in love, shapes character and builds trust. Proverbs 13:22 adds, "A good man leaves an inheritance to his children's children." That inheritance is not just material—it's spiritual, emotional, and relational. Sons are meant to receive wisdom, faith, and identity from their fathers and carry it forward.

Ultimately, sonhood is a sacred calling. It's about being loved, being shaped, and being sent into purpose. Whether in earthly families or in our relationship with God, sonhood reflects the heart of the Father—a heart that longs to guide, restore, and bless.

Sonhood is a journey filled with complexity, emotion, and transformation. While the Bible gives us timeless truths about the role of sons and fathers, real-life stories bring those truths into sharper focus. Sons often carry silent burdens—questions about identity, longing for affirmation, and the deep desire to be seen and understood by their fathers. When fatherhood is present and intentional, sons flourish. But when it's absent or fractured, the effects can ripple through a lifetime.

There are stories of sons who grew up without their fathers entirely. Some found mentors or spiritual fathers who stepped in to fill the gap. Others struggled with identity, anger, or a sense of abandonment. In these cases, the absence of fatherhood often led to a search for belonging—sometimes in healthy communities, other times in destructive patterns. The consequences of fatherlessness are real: increased vulnerability to mental health challenges, difficulty forming stable relationships, and a deep internal question— "Am I enough?"

Yet, there are stories of healing. Sons who, despite broken beginnings, found restoration through faith, forgiveness, and intentional relationships. Some reconnected with their fathers later in life. Others became the kind of fathers they never had, determined to break the cycle. Sonhood is not static—it evolves. And with grace, even the most painful chapters can be rewritten.

Whether through biblical examples or modern testimonies, sonhood is a sacred identity. It's shaped by the presence—or absence—of fatherhood. And when nurtured with love, guidance, and spiritual truth, it becomes a foundation for legacy, healing, and purpose.

If you're reading this and you've had a complicated relationship with your parents, I want to say: you're not alone. Sonhood is messy. It's layered. It's full of joy and grief and everything in between. But it's also redemptive. There's always room for healing. Always room for reconnection. Always room for grace.

And if your parents are no longer here, know this: you still carry them. In your voice. In your habits. In your heart. You are their legacy. And you get to decide what that legacy becomes.

Sonhood is not a passive identity. It's an active calling. It's about remembering, honouring, forgiving, and becoming. It's about knowing where you come from, so you can know where you're going. And it's one of the things every man should know.

Chapter Six

HUSBANDHOOD

I didn't fully understand what it meant to be a husband until I was one. I had ideas, of course—some shaped by movies, some by my parents, some by my own hopes. I thought it meant being a provider, a protector, a partner. And it does. But it also means being a student. A servant. A mirror. A witness.

Husbandhood is not a role you perform. It's a relationship you cultivate. It's not about getting everything right—it's about staying when it's hard, listening when it's quiet, and loving when it's inconvenient.

I remember the early days of marriage – got married in 1990. Everything felt new and exciting. We were learning each other's rhythms, discovering quirks, building routines. There was laughter, intimacy, adventure. But there were also misunderstandings. Arguments over small things that somehow felt big. Moments of silence that felt heavier than words. And I realized quickly: love isn't just a feeling. It's a choice. A daily one.

Being a husband means choosing your partner again and again. Not just on the good days, but on the ordinary ones. The tired ones. The tense ones. It means showing up when you'd rather shut down. It means leaning in when you feel like pulling away.

I've learned that communication is the lifeblood of husbandhood. Not just talking but listening. Not just hearing words but understanding emotions. My wife doesn't always need me to fix things—sometimes she just needs me to be present. To sit with her in the mess. To say, "I see you. I'm with you."

That kind of presence takes humility. It takes patience. It takes the willingness to put your ego aside and ask, "What does love require of me right now?"

I've failed at that more times than I can count. I've been distracted, defensive, dismissive. I've let stress spill into our conversations. I've let pride keep me from apologizing. But every time I've chosen humility— every time I've said, "I was wrong," or "I'm sorry," or "Help me understand"—our bond has deepened.

The Bible speaks with great clarity and tenderness about the role of a husband, not as a ruler or enforcer, but as a servant-leader, a protector, and a lover who mirrors Christ's love for the Church. Being a husband is not just about fulfilling duties—it's about embodying grace, patience, and sacrificial love. And when you come from a difficult cultural or ethnic background, with traditions that may clash or challenge unity, the biblical model becomes even more vital. It teaches us that love must be the foundation, not dominance, not pride, and certainly not unresolved conflict.

Ephesians 5:25 sets the tone: "Husbands, love your wives, just as Christ loved the church and gave himself up for her." That's not casual affection—it's radical, self-giving love. Christ laid down His life for the Church, and husbands are called to love with that same depth. It means choosing unity over ego, tenderness over control, and forgiveness over resentment.

Colossians 3:19 adds, "Husbands, love your wives and do not be harsh with them." This verse speaks directly to the emotional climate of a marriage. In cultures where men are taught to be stoic or dominant, this command is countercultural. It calls husbands to be gentle, understanding, and emotionally present. It's not weakness—it's strength under control.

1 Peter 3:7 continues this theme: "Husbands, in the same way, be considerate as you live with your wives, and treat them with respect… so that nothing will hinder your prayers." This verse links spiritual health to relational health. When a husband honours his wife, listens to her, and treats her as an equal partner, it reflects God's heart—and it opens the door to deeper spiritual intimacy.

Genesis 2:24 reminds us of the original design: "A man shall leave his father and mother and be united to his wife, and they shall become one flesh." That "oneness" is not automatic—it's cultivated. And when two people come from different traditions, languages, or expectations, becoming one requires humility, intentionality, and a whole lot of grace. You and your wife Kathleen chose love over division, and that's exactly what Scripture calls us to do. Love is the glue that holds the differences together.

Your journey of learning how to become one—through cultural tension, differing opinions, and the challenges of blending backgrounds—is a living testimony of biblical marriage. It's not about perfection; it's about perseverance. It's about choosing love when it's hard, and letting God shape you both through the process.

The Bible doesn't give us a one-size-fits-all template for marriage, but it does give us timeless principles: love sacrificially, lead spiritually, honour consistently, and forgive freely. When those truths guide a marriage, even the most difficult backgrounds can become fertile ground for growth, healing, and joy.

Husbandhood is not about being the hero. It's about being the teammate. The co-builder. The co-dreamer. It's about creating a life together, not just surviving one.

There was a season when my wife was going through something heavy—emotionally, spiritually. I didn't know how to help. I felt helpless. But I learned that sometimes, the most loving thing you can do is stay close. Not with answers, but with empathy. Not with solutions, but with solidarity. That's husbandhood. It's the ministry of presence.

It's also the practice of celebration. Of noticing the good. Of speaking life. I've learned that my words carry weight. A compliment can lift her spirit. A kind note can shift her day. A moment of gratitude can soften a week of stress.

I try to say "thank you" often. Not just for the big things, but for the small ones. For the way she laughs at my jokes. For the meals she cooks. For the way she loves our children. For the way she forgives me. Gratitude is fuel for love.

Husbandhood also means growing together. We're not the same people we were when we got married. Life has changed us. Parenthood has stretched us. Loss has shaped us. And through it all, we've had to keep choosing each other. Keep teaching each other. Keep loving each other.

There are days when we feel distant. When the connection feels thin. When the spark feels dim. And in those moments, I've learned not to panic—but to pursue. To ask questions. To plan a date. To write a note.

To initiate a hug. Love doesn't always reignite on its own. Sometimes, you have to strike the match.

I've also learned that husbandhood is spiritual. It's not just emotional or practical—it's sacred. It's a reflection of something divine. To love someone fully, to serve them selflessly, to forgive them endlessly—that's holy work.

And it's hard work. But it's worth it.

If you're a husband reading this, I want to say: you matter. Your love matters. Your presence matters. You don't have to be perfect. You just have to be intentional.

And if you're not yet a husband, or never will be, know this: the heart of husbandhood is not limited to marriage. It's about commitment. It's about love. It's about choosing to build something beautiful with someone else.

Husbandhood is not a title. It's a calling. And it's one of the things every man should know.

CHAPTER SIX : HUSBANDHOOD

Chapter Seven

THE STRUGGLES MEN FACE

I've wrestled with confidence for most of my life. Not the kind that shows up in job interviews or social gatherings, but the quiet kind—the kind that lives inside you or doesn't. The kind that lets you walk into a room without needing to prove anything. The kind that lets you speak without second-guessing every word. The kind that lets you look in the mirror and say, "I'm enough."

For years, I didn't feel that way. I felt like I was always auditioning. For approval. For respect. For belonging. I'd walk into meetings and wonder if I was smart enough. I'd go on dates and wonder if I was interesting enough. I'd sit with friends and wonder if I was funny enough. And underneath all of that was a deeper question I didn't know how to ask: Am I worthy?

Confidence, I've learned, isn't about being the loudest voice in the room. It's about being the truest. It's about knowing who you are and being okay with it. But getting there takes work. It takes unlearning the lies you've believed about yourself. It takes healing the wounds you've buried. It takes facing the fear that maybe, just maybe, you're not enough.

I remember one season of my life when I felt completely lost. I had just left a job after building it up and moved into another region to start the same type of job working in crisis with the police and hospitals. I didn't know what was next. I didn't know who I was without the title, the routine, the sense of purpose. I woke up every morning with a pit in my stomach. I felt like I was drifting. And the worst part was, I didn't know how to talk about it. I didn't want to seem weak. I didn't want to worry anyone. So, I smiled. I said I was fine. And inside, I was falling apart.

That's one of the struggles men faces—silence. We're taught to be strong, to be stoic, to be self-sufficient. We're taught that emotions are dangerous, that vulnerability is weakness, that asking for help is failure. So we carry our pain in private. We bury our fears. We numb our wounds. And we wonder why we feel so alone.

I've had moments where I wanted to cry but couldn't. Not because I didn't feel anything, but because I didn't know how to let it out. I'd sit in my car after a long day, staring at the steering wheel, feeling the weight of everything I couldn't say. And I'd think, "Is this what being a man is supposed to feel like?"

Lonely. Heavy. Silent. But it doesn't have to be.

I've learned that strength isn't about holding it all together. It's about knowing when to let go. When to speak. When to ask for help. When to say, "I'm not okay." That kind of strength doesn't come naturally. It has to be chosen. Practiced. Protected.

Another struggle I've faced is comparison. I look around and see men who seem to have it all—success, confidence, families, purpose. And I wonder, "What am I missing?" I scroll through social media and see curated lives that make mine feel small. I hear stories of achievement and feel like I'm falling behind. And I forget that everyone is fighting a battle I can't see.

Comparison is a thief. It steals joy. It steals gratitude. It steals presence. It convinces you that your life isn't enough, that your story isn't valuable, that your worth is measured by someone else's highlight reel. I've had to learn to stay in my lane. To honour my journey. To trust that I'm exactly where I need to be, even if it doesn't look like someone else's path.

Relationships have brought their own struggles. I've loved deeply and lost painfully. I've said things I wish I could take back. I've stayed silent when I should have spoken. I've let pride get in the way of connection. And I've learned that intimacy requires courage. It requires honesty. It requires the willingness to be seen—not just the polished version, but the real one.

There was a time when I thought love was about performance. About being impressive. About being strong. But real love—lasting love—is about being known. And that's terrifying. What if I'm not enough? What if I am not doing what is being expected?

I am grateful to God that in my journey of trials and errors, Kathleen never walked away or say she had enough. There are regrets of choosing to be the only voice in the relationship and making most of the decisions. But maturity and time has taught me to think different.

I've also learned that love is where healing happens. In the presence of someone who sees you and stays. In the safety of a relationship where you can be flawed and still loved. That kind of love doesn't just change your relationship—it changes you.

Fatherhood brought its own set of struggles. The pressure to provide. The fear of failing. The weight of shaping another human life. I've had nights where I lay awake wondering if I'm doing enough. If I'm present enough. If I'm loving enough. And I've had to remind myself that being a good father isn't about perfection—it's about presence. It's about showing up, again and again, even when you're tired, even when you're unsure, even when you feel like you're failing.

I've also struggled with purpose. With the question, "Why am I here?" I've chased careers, dreams, goals—hoping they'd fill the void. And sometimes they did. For a while. But eventually, the emptiness returned. Because purpose isn't found in achievement. It's found in alignment. In living a life that reflects your values. In doing work that matters. In loving people well.

There was a moment when I realized that my purpose wasn't something I had to find—it was something I had to live. In the way I treat my family. In the way I show up for my friends. In the way I serve my community. In the way I carry myself when no one's watching.

I've struggled with identity. With the question, "Who am I?" Not just what I do, or what I've accomplished, or what others think of me— but who I am at my core. That question has haunted me at times. Especially in seasons of transition. When the roles I've played no longer fit. When the masks I've worn start to crack. When the noise of the world drowns out the voice inside me.

I've learned that identity isn't something you earn—it's something you uncover. It's found in silence. In solitude. In reflection. It's found in the moments when you stop performing and start becoming.

The struggles men face is real. They're deep. They're often hidden. But they're not shameful. They're human. And the more we talk about them, the more we heal. The more we connect. The more we grow.

Life can be incredibly complicated for men, especially when it comes to the quiet battles they often fight alone. There's a constant tug-of-war between who they are, who they're expected to be, and what they feel deep inside. Many of these struggles—lust, sex, pornography, gambling, negativity, crime—aren't just random behaviours. They're often symptoms of something deeper, something aching beneath the surface.

Lust and sexual temptation, for instance, can feel overpowering. It's not just about desire—it's about validation, escape, and sometimes even loneliness. Pornography, in particular, offers a quick fix, a momentary sense of control or pleasure, but it can quietly chip away at a man's ability to connect deeply with others. Over time, it can distort how intimacy is understood and make real relationships feel distant or even intimidating. Many men don't talk about this because they feel ashamed, but the truth is, it's more common than most people realize.

Gambling is another escape. It starts with thrill and excitement, but for some, it becomes a way to numb pain or chase a sense of worth. The highs and lows mimic emotional cycles—hope, despair, adrenaline—and when life feels out of control, gambling can offer the illusion of power. But it's fleeting, and the consequences can be devastating, not just financially but emotionally too.

Negativity often creeps in quietly. It can look like anger, sarcasm, or withdrawal, but underneath it is usually hurt, disappointment, or fear. Many men are taught to be strong, to push through, to never show weakness. So instead of expressing sadness or vulnerability, they bottle it up, and it leaks out in ways that damage their relationships and their sense of self.

Getting involved with the wrong crowd, stealing, or committing crimes often stems from a need to belong or to be seen. When a man feels invisible, rejected, or powerless, he might seek out people who offer a sense of identity—even if it's built on unhealthy foundations.

Sometimes it's about survival, sometimes rebellion, and sometimes it's just about feeling alive in a world that feels numb.

All these struggles have roots. They grow from places like childhood wounds, broken homes, unmet emotional needs, or environments that never taught healthy ways to cope. When there's no safe space to talk, no one to listen without judgment, men often turn inward or outward in destructive ways. But these behaviours don't define them. They're signals—cries for help, for healing, for connection.

What's needed isn't more shame or silence. It's compassion, understanding, and the courage to face these struggles head-on. Healing begins when men are given permission to feel, to speak, and to be seen—not just for their mistakes, but for their humanity.

The Bible speaks with deep compassion and honesty about the struggles men face. It doesn't shy away from the reality of hardship, temptation, or failure—in fact, it often presents them as part of the journey toward growth, faith, and transformation. Struggle is not seen as a sign of weakness, but as a refining fire that can shape character and deepen trust in God.

One of the most comforting truths in Scripture is that God doesn't abandon people in their pain. In James 1:2–3, it says, "Consider it pure joy… whenever you face trials of many kinds, because you know that the testing of your faith produces perseverance." That verse doesn't suggest that suffering is easy—it acknowledges that trials are real—but it also reminds us that there's purpose in the pain. Struggles can build endurance, and endurance can shape a man into someone stronger, wiser, and more grounded.

Romans 5:3–4 echoes this idea: "We also glory in our sufferings, because we know that suffering produces perseverance; perseverance, character; and character, hope." There's a progression here—struggle leads to growth, and growth leads to hope. It's a reminder that even when life feels heavy, there's a future worth pressing toward.

The Bible also speaks to the emotional weight men carry. In 1 Peter 5:10, it says, "After you have suffered a little while, [God] will Himself restore you and make you strong, firm and steadfast." That's a promise of healing—not just physical, but emotional and spiritual restoration. God sees the weariness, the temptations, the battles with lust, anger, or loneliness, and He offers strength in return.

Men like David, Moses, Elijah, and Paul all faced deep struggles—some battled fear, others wrestled with failure, temptation, or rejection. Yet their stories were not defined by their lowest moments. They were shaped by how they turned back to God, how they allowed grace to meet them in their brokenness.

So, when a man feels overwhelmed, tempted, or lost, the Bible doesn't condemn him—it invites him to come closer to God. To lean into grace. To remember that he's not alone, and that even in the darkest valley, there's a Shepherd walking beside him.

If you're reading this and you feel the weight of these struggles, I want you to know you're not alone. You're not broken. You're not weak. You're a man in progress. A man becoming. A man worthy of love, of healing, of purpose.

CHAPTER SEVEN : THE STRUGGLES MEN FACE

Chapter Eight

INSECURITIES

I've spent a lot of my life trying to outrun my insecurities. I thought if I worked hard enough, achieved enough, looked good enough, or acted confident enough, they'd eventually disappear. But they didn't. They just got quieter, more subtle, more clever. They didn't shout anymore—they whispered. And sometimes, those whispers were louder than anything else.

Insecurity is a strange thing. It doesn't always show up as fear. Sometimes it shows up as arrogance. As overcompensation. As perfectionism. As withdrawal. I've worn all those masks. I've tried to be the smartest guy in the room, the most agreeable, the most capable. Not because I was proud—but because I was afraid. Afraid of being seen. Afraid of being judged. Afraid of not being enough.

I remember being in a meeting once, surrounded by people I respected. I had ideas. Good ones. But I didn't speak. I sat there, nodding, pretending to be engaged, while inside I was battling a voice that said, "Don't embarrass yourself. You're not qualified. You'll sound stupid." That voice didn't come from nowhere. It came from years of self-doubt. From moments in childhood when I felt overlooked. From relationships where I felt misunderstood. From a culture that told me I had to be flawless to be valuable.

That's the thing about insecurity—it's rarely logical. It's emotional. It's historical. It's layered. And it doesn't go away just because you tell it to.

I've had insecurities about my body. About my intelligence. About my masculinity. About my worth. I've looked in the mirror and picked myself apart. I've replayed conversations and criticized every word. I've walked into rooms and felt like I didn't belong. And I've smiled through all of it, hoping no one would notice.

But they did. Because insecurity leaks. It shows up in how you carry yourself. In how you speak. In how you love. In how you lead. It shows up in the way you hesitate, the way you deflect, the way you shrink.

I've learned that the only way to deal with insecurity is to face it. To name it. To sit with it. To ask, "Where did you come from?" And then, slowly, to rewrite the story.

I had a conversation with a close friend once. I told him I often felt like I wasn't enough. That no matter what I did, I always felt like I was falling short. He looked at me and said, "You don't have to earn your worth. You already have it." I didn't believe him at first. But I let those words sink in. And over time, they started to heal something in me.

Insecurity thrives in isolation. It grows in silence. But when you speak it—when you bring it into the light—it loses power. That's why relationships matter. That's why honesty matters. That's why vulnerability matters.

I've also learned that insecurity isn't something to be ashamed of. It's part of being human. Every man I've ever known—no matter how successful, confident, or composed—has wrestled with it. Some just hide it better than others.

There was a time when I thought being a man meant being unshakable. But now I know it means being honest. It means being willing to say, "I struggle with this." It means being brave enough to ask for help. It means being strong enough to admit weakness.

I've had to unlearn a lot of things. That my value isn't tied to my performance. That my worth isn't measured by my appearance. That my masculinity isn't defined by dominance. That my identity isn't dependent on others' approval.

And I've had to learn new things. That I am loved. That I am enough. That I am growing. That I am allowed to be imperfect.

Insecurity doesn't disappear overnight. It shows up in waves. But now, when it does, I don't run. I don't hide. I don't pretend. I breathe. I reflect. I reach out. I remind myself of the truth.

Insecurity is something that quietly creeps into our hearts. It can make us question our worth, doubt our abilities, and feel like we're not enough—no matter how hard we try. Sometimes it comes from past wounds, words spoken over us, or comparisons we make with others. Other times, it's just the weight of expectations we carry, trying to be strong, successful, or accepted. It's a lonely feeling, and it can make even the brightest moments feel dim.

But the Bible speaks gently and powerfully to those places of insecurity. It reminds us that we are not defined by our fears or failures, but by the love of a God who sees us fully and still chooses us. One verse that brings comfort is Isaiah 41:10, where God says, "Fear not, for I am with you; be not dismayed, for I am your God. I will strengthen you and help you." That's not just a promise—it's a personal reassurance that we're never walking alone, even when we feel uncertain or small.

Psalm 139:14 tells us that we are "fearfully and wonderfully made." That means our value isn't based on how we look, what we achieve, or how others see us. It's rooted in the fact that we were crafted with care and intention. Even when we feel overlooked or inadequate, God sees beauty and purpose in us.

Insecurity often whispers lies, but Scripture speaks truth. In 2 Timothy 1:7, we're reminded that "God has not given us a spirit of fear, but of power and of love and of a sound mind." That means we're equipped—not just to survive, but to live with confidence and clarity. When insecurity tries to take hold, we can lean into that truth and remember who we are and whose we are.

The Bible doesn't ignore our struggles—it meets them with grace. It invites us to bring our doubts, our fears, and our fragile places to God, who doesn't turn away but draws near. Insecurity may be part of the journey, but it doesn't have to be the destination. There's healing, strength, and peace waiting for us when we choose to trust the One who made us and walks with us every step of the way.

If you're reading this and you feel the weight of insecurity, I want you to know: you're not alone. You're not broken. You're not weak. You're human. And you're worthy.

You don't have to be perfect to be loved. You don't have to be fearless to be strong. You don't have to be impressive to be enough.

You just have to be you. And that's something every man should know.

Chapter Nine

SOCIAL AWKWARDNESS

I've often felt like I didn't quite fit in when I was around other people. There's this quiet discomfort that follows me into social settings, like I'm always slightly out of sync with the room. Part of it comes from my skin colour and ethnic background—things that make me visibly different, and sometimes feel like I'm being silently judged or misunderstood before I even speak. It's not always overt, but it's there, lingering in the way people look, react, or exclude without meaning to.

I've also struggled with feeling like I'm not as intelligent as others. In conversations, I sometimes second-guess myself, wondering if I sound naive or if I'm falling short of the sharpness and confidence others seem to carry so effortlessly. That feeling of being mentally outmatched can be isolating, especially when it seems like everyone else is effortlessly keeping up.

Then there's the pressure of appearance—of not being as popular or attractive as the people who seem to glide through life with charm and ease. I look at magazines or social media and see these polished, confident faces, and I can't help but feel like I'm on the outside looking in. I don't look like the guys in GQ, and sometimes that makes me question my own worth, like I'm missing some invisible standard that everyone else seems to meet.

All of these feelings—being different, being less, being overlooked—can build up over time. They don't just affect how I see others; they shape how I see myself. But I'm learning that these struggles don't define me. They're part of my story, yes, but they're not the whole story. There's strength in being different, and there's beauty in being real. I'm still figuring it out, still growing, but I'm trying to give myself grace in the process.

I'd walk into a party or a networking event and feel like I was wearing the wrong skin. Everyone else seemed to know what to say, how to stand, when to laugh. I'd hover near the edges, pretending to check my phone, hoping someone would start a conversation so I wouldn't have to.

It wasn't that I didn't want connection. I did. Deeply. But something about those environments made me shrink. I'd rehearse lines in my head, second-guess my tone, worry about being boring. And when I did speak, I'd analyze every word afterward, wondering if I'd come off as weird or awkward or forgettable.

Social awkwardness isn't always visible. It's not loud. It's not dramatic. It's subtle. It's the hesitation before you speak. The overthinking after you do. The quiet panic when someone asks, "So, what do you do?" and your mind goes blank. It's the feeling of being on the outside, even when you're standing in the middle of the room.

I used to think I was the only one who felt this way. But over time, I started opening up to other men—friends, coworkers, mentors—and I realized something: I wasn't alone. So many of us carry this discomfort. We just hide it well. We mask it with humor, with confidence, with silence. But underneath, we're all just trying to figure out how to belong.

There was a season in my life when I avoided social situations altogether. I told myself I was too busy, too tired, too uninterested. But the truth was, I was afraid. Afraid of being judged. Afraid of being misunderstood. Afraid of being invisible. And the more I avoided, the lonelier I became.

One night, a friend invited me to a small gathering. Just a few guys, nothing formal. I almost said no. But something in me said, "Go" and my wife Kathleen encouraged me to go. So I did. And it was awkward at first. I didn't know anyone. I didn't know what to say. But then someone cracked a joke. Someone else shared a story. And slowly, the tension eased. I started talking. I started listening. I started laughing. And by the end of the night, I felt something I hadn't felt in a long time: connected.

That night didn't cure my social awkwardness. But it reminded me that connection is possible. That belonging isn't about being perfect— it's about being present.

I've learned that social awkwardness often comes from fear. Fear of rejection. Fear of judgment. Fear of not measuring up. And the only way to move through that fear is to face it. To show up anyway. To speak anyway. To risk being seen.

I've also learned that awkwardness isn't a flaw. It's a sign that you care. That you're paying attention. That you're trying. And that's something to honour, not hide.

There are still moments when I feel out of place. When I stumble over my words. When I misread a cue. When I leave a conversation feeling unsure. But now, I don't beat myself up. I breathe. I reflect. I remind myself that I'm growing.

And I've found that the more I embrace my awkwardness, the more others do too. When I'm honest about my discomfort, it gives others permission to be honest about theirs. And suddenly, the room feels safer. The conversation feels deeper. The connection feels real.

Social awkwardness doesn't mean you're broken. It means you're human. It means you're learning. It means you're brave enough to keep showing up, even when it's hard.

If you're reading this and you feel socially awkward, I want you to know you're not alone. You're not strange. You're not failing. You're just navigating a world that doesn't always make space for quiet souls. But your voice matters. Your presence matters. Your story matters.

You don't have to be the life of the party to be valuable. You don't have to be smooth or witty or charismatic. You just have to be you. And that's something every man should know.

Chapter Ten

CONNECTION AND BOUNDARIES

I've always wanted to connect deeply with others. Not just surface-level friendships or polite conversations, but real connection—the kind that makes you feel seen, heard, understood. But for a long time, I didn't know how to do that without losing myself. I'd either hold back too much or give away too much. I'd either build walls or forget to build any at all.

Connection, I've learned, is not just about openness. It's about wisdom. It's about knowing when to lean in and when to step back. It's about recognizing your own emotional landscape and honouring it, even as you try to understand someone else's.

There was a time when I thought being a good man meant being available to everyone. I said yes to every request, every conversation, every emotional need. I didn't want to disappoint anyone. I didn't want to seem selfish. But over time, I started to feel drained. I started to feel resentful. I started to feel like I was disappearing in the name of connection.

For a long time, I found it difficult to connect with other men. There was this invisible wall I couldn't seem to climb—built from fear, insecurity, and the belief that I had to always be strong, silent, and self-sufficient. I grew up thinking vulnerability was something you kept hidden, especially around other guys. So, I kept my distance. I'd smile, nod, make small talk, but never let anyone in too close.

But deep down, I craved connection. Not just surface-level friendships, but real, honest relationships where I could be myself—flawed, uncertain, and human. The turning point came when I realized that fear was keeping me isolated. I had to push through it, even when it felt unnatural.

I remember one time at a men's retreat. I almost didn't go. I had every excuse lined up—too busy, too tired, not my thing. But my wife Kathleen strongly suggested for me to, "Just show up." So, I did. And I sat in a circle with strangers who looked like they had it all together. I felt like an outsider. But then one man shared about his struggles with depression and how he felt like he was failing as a father. His honesty cracked something open in me. I found myself speaking up, sharing things I'd never said out loud before in a personal level. It was different in speaking as a therapy. And instead of judgment, I was met with nods, tears, and quiet understanding. That moment changed me.

Another time, I reached out to a guy I'd known for years but never really talked to beyond casual greetings. I invited him for coffee. It felt awkward at first—two men sitting across from each other, unsure of what to say. But slowly, the conversation deepened. We talked about our fears, our dreams, our regrets. That coffee turned into a friendship that's still growing today.

I had been working out at the gym for over a year before I finally built up the courage to say hello to one guy who always seemed to know exactly what he was doing. His name was Daniel. To my surprise, when I greeted him, he smiled and said, "What took you so long?" That simple moment broke the ice, and not long after, we became gym buddies.

Daniel started showing me proper techniques—how to structure my workouts, how to maintain good posture during lifts, and how to train with intention. I began to notice changes in my body, slowly shaping and strengthening in ways I hadn't achieved before. His guidance made a real difference, not just physically but mentally too.

We became a familiar duo at the gym. Most of the regulars who worked out in the morning recognized us, and there was a sense of camaraderie that grew around that shared space. Our workouts were fun and energizing, but they also became a time for deeper conversations. We talked about life, struggles, goals, and everything in between. That connection reminded me how powerful it can be to push past fear and reach out—sometimes, the friendships we need are just one "hello" away.

What I've learned is that connection doesn't come from pretending to be perfect. It comes from showing up as you are. Men are often taught to compete, to compare, to keep emotions tucked away. But when we choose to be real—with our pain, our doubts, our hopes—we give others permission to do the same. And that's where true brotherhood begins.

It's not always easy. Sometimes I still feel that old fear creeping in. But I remind myself that courage isn't the absence of fear—it's moving forward in spite of it. Every time I've leaned into discomfort and reached out, I've found something meaningful on the other side.

For most of my life, connecting with other men felt like walking into a room where everyone spoke a language I didn't quite understand. There was this unspoken code—be tough, be cool, don't show weakness. And I tried to follow it, even when it didn't feel natural. I'd keep conversations light, avoid anything too personal, and convince myself that I didn't need close male friendships. But deep down, I knew I was missing something. I longed for connection, for brotherhood, for the kind of relationships where I could be fully seen and still accepted.

The fear of rejection was real. I worried that if I opened up, I'd be judged or misunderstood. I thought maybe I wasn't "man enough" to belong. That fear kept me quiet in rooms full of laughter, kept me distant in groups where I desperately wanted to feel included. But eventually, I realized that fear was costing me more than it was protecting me. So I started doing the hard thing—reaching out.

I've learned that men are often starving for connection but afraid to admit it. We're taught to compete, to compare, to keep our emotions tucked away. But when we choose to be real—with our pain, our doubts, our hopes—we give others permission to do the same. And that's where true brotherhood begins. It's not about fixing each other. It's about walking alongside each other.

I've also discovered that connection doesn't always come naturally. Sometimes you have to fight for it. You have to show up even when it's uncomfortable. You must ask the deeper questions, share the harder truths, and be willing to sit in silence when words don't come. But every time I've done that, I've found something meaningful on the other side.

That's when I began to learn about boundaries.

Boundaries aren't walls. They're doors. They're the way we teach others how to treat us. They're the way we protect our energy, our values, our time. They're the way we stay whole while still being open.

I remember a friendship that pushed me to my limits. He was going through a hard time, and I wanted to be there for him. I listened, supported, encouraged. But it became one-sided. He'd call at all hours, unload everything, and never ask how I was doing. I didn't say anything for a while—I didn't want to seem uncaring. But eventually, I realized I was carrying more than I could hold. I had to speak up. I had to say, "I care about you, but I need space too."

It was hard. He didn't take it well at first. But it was honest. And it was necessary.

As men, we're often taught to be strong, to be dependable, to be the rock. But even rocks crack under pressure. We need boundaries not because we're weak, but because we're human.

I've learned that connection thrives when boundaries are clear. When both people know where they stand. When there's mutual respect, mutual effort, mutual care. Without boundaries, connection becomes obligation. It becomes imbalance. It becomes unsustainable.

There are days when I'm emotionally spent. Days when I need solitude more than conversation. Days when I need to say no, even to people I love. And I've learned to honour those days. To trust that real connection doesn't require constant availability—it requires authenticity.

I've had to learn how to say things like: "I'm not in a place to talk right now." "I care about you, but I need time to process." "I want to support you, but I need to take care of myself too."

Those words used to feel selfish. Now they feel sacred.

Connection also requires self-awareness. I've had to ask myself hard questions: Why do I feel responsible for everyone's emotions? Why do I avoid conflict? Why do I feel guilty when I set boundaries?

The answers weren't easy. They came from old wounds, old patterns, old beliefs. But facing them helped me grow. Helped me connect more honestly. Helped me love more freely.

I've found that the best connections come from men who know themselves. Who aren't afraid to say, "This is where I end and you begin." Who can be present without being consumed. Who can love without losing themselves.

There's a quiet strength in that kind of connection. It's not flashy. It's not dramatic. It's steady. It's safe. It's real.

I've also learned that boundaries aren't just about protecting myself—they're about protecting the relationship. When I'm clear about what I can offer, I'm less likely to resent. When I'm honest about what I need, I'm more likely to stay engaged. When I respect my limits, I'm more able to love well.

With boundaries, I've learned that limitations are important. For a long time, I thought saying "no" meant I was letting people down. I believed that setting limits made me selfish or weak, especially when others seemed to expect me to always be available, always helpful, always agreeable. But over time, I learned that honouring my own boundaries wasn't a betrayal of others—it was an act of self-respect.

One of the first times I really had to set a limit was with a friend who constantly leaned on me for emotional support. I cared about him deeply, but the calls were daily, sometimes late at night, and always heavy. I started to feel drained, like I was carrying someone else's weight without any room to breathe. I wrestled with guilt—what kind of friend pulls back when someone's hurting? But I realized I wasn't helping him by burning myself out. So I gently told him I needed to take a step back, that I was struggling too and needed space to recharge. It wasn't easy. I worried he'd be upset or feel abandoned. But to my surprise, he understood. And I felt a sense of relief I hadn't felt in months.

Another time, I was asked to take on a project at work that I knew would stretch me too thin. My instinct was to say yes—I didn't want to seem incapable or uncommitted. But I paused and asked myself what the cost would be. I had other responsibilities, and I was already feeling overwhelmed. So I said no. Politely, respectfully, but firmly. And again, the world didn't collapse. The project was reassigned, and I was able to focus on what I could handle without sacrificing my mental health.

Setting limits isn't about shutting people out. It's about knowing your capacity and protecting your peace. It's recognizing that you can't pour from an empty cup. I've learned that when I honour my boundaries, I show up more fully in the areas that matter most. I'm more present, more grounded, and more authentic.

There are still moments when I feel that old guilt creeping in. But I remind myself that boundaries are not walls—they're doors. They let in what's healthy and keep out what's harmful. And the more I practice setting them, the more I trust myself to know what I need and when I need it.

So if you're someone who struggles with saying no, or feels guilty for needing space, I want you to know it's okay. You're allowed to protect your energy. You're allowed to choose rest over obligation. And you're allowed to be kind to yourself, even if it means disappointing someone else for a moment. Because in the long run, honouring your limits helps you stay whole. And that's something worth holding onto.

Connection is a dance. It requires rhythm. It requires listening. It requires knowing when to step forward and when to step back. And the more I practice, the more graceful I become.

If you're a man reading this and you struggle with connection, I want you to know: it's okay. You're not broken. You're not cold. You're learning. And the fact that you care means you're already on the right path.

Start by knowing yourself. What fills you? What drains you? What do you need to feel safe, seen, supported?

Then, speak it. Kindly. Clearly. Consistently. And trust that the right people will honour it. Connection isn't about being everything. It's about being true.

Chapter Eleven

SEX AND DESIRE

Sex has always been a complicated subject for me. Not because I didn't feel desire—if anything, I felt it too strongly—but because I didn't know what to do with it. I didn't know how to talk about it. I didn't know how to understand it. I didn't know how to separate it from shame, from pressure, from confusion.

Growing up, I was taught that having a strong sex drive was normal for a man. Expected, even. It was joked about, glorified, sometimes even weaponized. But no one ever taught me how to handle it with wisdom. No one taught me how to honour it. No one taught me how to connect it to love, to intimacy, to emotional depth.

Sex is powerful. It's beautiful. It's sacred. But it's also vulnerable. And when we don't understand it—when we don't talk about it—it can become a source of struggle instead of strength.

I've wrestled with guilt around my desires when I was a teenager and young adult. Times when I felt like they were too strong, too distracting, too consuming. I've felt ashamed for wanting, for fantasizing, for feeling. And I've had to unlearn the belief that desire is dirty. That sex is something to hide. That being a man means being constantly hungry and barely in control.

There were moments in my marriage when I felt disconnected during intimacy. Moments when I was physically present but emotionally absent. Moments when I was trying to prove something instead of share something. And afterward, I'd feel empty. Not because the experience was bad, but because it wasn't whole.

I've learned that sex without emotional connection can leave you lonelier than before. It can feel like closeness, but it doesn't always heal. It doesn't always satisfy. It doesn't always speak to the deeper parts of you. Sex with your spouse needs to be magical, focused, intentional and emotionally connected.

That's one of the struggles men face—we're taught to separate sex from emotion. To pursue pleasure without vulnerability. To seek satisfaction without intimacy. And then we wonder why we feel disconnected, misunderstood, unfulfilled.

I've had to learn what sex is. Not just biologically, but relationally. Spiritually. Emotionally. I've had to learn that it's not just about desire—it's about trust. It's about safety. It's about being fully present, fully known, fully accepted.

That kind of sex doesn't start in the bedroom. It starts in conversation. In honesty. In emotional availability. And that's hard. Because it means facing your fears. It means naming your insecurities. It means asking for what you need, even when you're afraid you won't get it.

I've also had to confront my own limitations. Times when my sex drive didn't match my wife's. Times when stress or anxiety affected my body. Times when I felt disconnected from myself and couldn't connect with anyone else. Those moments were humbling. They made me question my worth. My masculinity. My identity.

But they also taught me grace. They taught me that being a man isn't about being invincible—it's about being honest. It's about being gentle with yourself. It's about learning to love in ways that go beyond performance.

I've had conversations with other men who've shared similar struggles. Men who feel ashamed of their desires. Men who feel pressure to always be ready, always be strong, always be in control. Men who feel confused about what it means to be sexual and still be emotionally grounded.

And every time we talk, there's healing. Because the silence breaks. Because the shame lifts. Because the truth comes out.

Sex is part of being human. It's not something to conquer—it's something to understand. It's not something to hide—it's something to honour. And the more we talk about it, the more we grow.

Sex is one of the most powerful forces in human experience, and it's no surprise that it's become a multibillion-dollar industry. From advertising to entertainment, from fashion to pharmaceuticals, the world has found countless ways to monetize desire. But behind all the numbers and flashy images is something deeply human—a longing for connection, pleasure, affirmation, and intimacy. For men, this longing often feels urgent and physical, driven by biology, emotion, and the need to feel close to someone they love.

Men tend to experience arousal externally. Visual cues, touch, and physical closeness can spark desire quickly. Women, on the other hand, often experience arousal more internally—through emotional connection, feeling safe, and being understood. This difference can create tension in marriages, especially when men feel physically drawn to their wives, but their wives interpret that desire as "just wanting sex." It's painful when a man feels rejected not just sexually, but emotionally, because his longing is misunderstood.

I've heard men reaching out for a hug, a cuddle, or a moment of closeness, and it was met with hesitation or avoidance. Not because their wives didn't care, but because their wives feared that any physical touch would lead to sex—and that sex was all they wanted. But that isn't true. Men want connection. Men wanted to feel close, to feel chosen, to feel like they mattered. Yes, physical intimacy can lead to sex, but it doesn't have to. Snuggling, holding hands, lying together in silence—these are all forms of intimacy that nourish a relationship.

Some women are afraid to engage physically because they've been taught that men are always thinking about sex. And while it's true that men often feel a strong sexual drive, it's not just about the act—it's about feeling bonded, desired, and emotionally safe. That drive is God-given. It's part of how men were created—to populate the earth, yes, but also to express love and unity in marriage. When used rightly, sexual desire is a beautiful and sacred part of a relationship. And when it's limited to one woman—your spouse—it becomes a powerful expression of commitment and trust.

But what happens when sex is absent in a marriage? It's a hard question, and one that many couples silently struggle with. The absence of sex can lead to feelings of rejection, loneliness, and even resentment. It can make a man question his worth, his attractiveness, and his place in the relationship. Over time, it can erode emotional intimacy and create distance that's hard to bridge.

In those moments, communication becomes essential. Not just about sex, but about feelings, fears, and needs. It's important to talk—not to accuse or demand, but to share honestly and listen deeply. Counselling can help, too. Sometimes there are deeper issues—emotional wounds, past trauma, or unmet needs—that need healing before physical intimacy can return.

And for the man who feels stuck in that silence, it's important to remember that your worth isn't defined by your sex life. You are still valuable, still loved, still capable of giving and receiving affection. Keep showing up with tenderness. Keep reaching out with patience. Keep honouring your spouse, even when it's hard. Because intimacy is built not just in the bedroom, but in the quiet moments of grace, understanding, and love.

When sex is absent in a marriage, it can feel like something sacred has gone missing. Not just the physical act, but the closeness, the warmth, the sense of being wanted and connected. For many couples, especially men, this absence can stir up confusion, frustration, and even grief. It's not just about unmet desire—it's about feeling emotionally distant from the person you've chosen to share your life with.

I've walked through seasons like this myself, where intimacy felt like a memory more than a reality. I remember lying beside my wife, both of us silent, the space between us heavy with things unsaid. I didn't know how to ask for what I needed without sounding selfish. She didn't know how to respond without feeling pressured. We were stuck in a quiet cycle of avoidance, and it hurt.

But I've learned that absence doesn't have to mean the end. It can be a signal—an invitation to pause, reflect, and rebuild. The first step is always communication. Not the kind that demands or accuses, but the kind that opens a door. Saying things like, "I miss you," or "I feel distant," can be more powerful than asking for sex directly. It's about naming the emotional gap, not just the physical one.

It's also important to understand that physical intimacy is layered. Cuddling, holding hands, gentle touch, even sitting close—these are all forms of connection that can lead to deeper intimacy. They're not sinful, and they're not manipulative. They're expressions of love. Sometimes, rebuilding sexual intimacy starts with simply being physically present in non-sexual ways. A hug that lingers. A hand on the back. A quiet moment of closeness without expectation.

In the Bible, sex within marriage is portrayed not only as a gift but as a sacred expression of love, unity, and covenant. It's a language of intimacy that speaks without words — a way for two people to say, "I belong to you, and you belong to me."

From the very beginning, God designed marriage to be a place of closeness and connection. In Genesis 2:24, we read, "Therefore a man shall leave his father and mother and be joined to his wife, and they shall become one flesh." That phrase — "one flesh" — is more than poetic. It's a picture of deep unity, physically and emotionally. Sex in marriage is part of that beautiful design. It's not shameful. It's not dirty. It's holy.

In the Song of Solomon, we see a celebration of romantic and sexual love between a husband and wife. The language is tender, passionate, and poetic. It reminds us that God is not embarrassed by desire — He created it. Within the safety of covenant, desire becomes a way to serve, cherish, and delight in one another.

Paul echoes this in 1 Corinthians 7, where he encourages spouses to care for each other's needs and to honour the mutual gift of their bodies. He writes, "The husband should fulfill his marital duty to his wife, and likewise the wife to her husband." This isn't about obligation — it's about generosity. It's about giving, not taking.

Sex in marriage is meant to be safe. It's a place where vulnerability is met with tenderness, not judgment. Hebrews 13:4 says, "Marriage should be honoured by all, and the marriage bed kept pure." This purity isn't just about avoiding sin — it's about protecting the sacredness of intimacy. It's about creating a space where love can flourish without fear.

For many, this topic brings up wounds — past mistakes, broken trust, or confusion. But the Bible also speaks of restoration. God is a healer. Whether you're newly married, rebuilding intimacy, or seeking understanding, His grace covers every part of your story. There is no shame in seeking help, asking questions, or growing together.

Sex in marriage is not just about pleasure — though that's part of the gift. It's about connection. It's about knowing and being known. It's about reflecting the love of Christ, who gave Himself fully for His bride, the Church.

If sex has been absent for a long time, it may be worth exploring why. Is there unresolved hurt? Exhaustion? Medical issues? Emotional disconnection? Therapy or counseling can help uncover these layers in a safe and guided way. Sometimes, just having a third party to help translate feelings can make all the difference.

And if you're the one feeling rejected, try not to internalize it as a reflection of your worth. It's easy to feel unattractive or unwanted, but often the issue isn't you—it's something your partner is carrying. Be patient, but also honest. You deserve intimacy, and your spouse does too.

Getting sex back into a marriage isn't about pressure—it's about presence. It's about showing up emotionally, spiritually, and physically. It's about rebuilding trust, rediscovering playfulness, and remembering that intimacy is a journey, not a transaction. And above all, it's about love—real, messy, vulnerable love that chooses connection even when it's hard.

So, if you're in that season, don't give up. Keep reaching out. Keep listening. Keep loving. Because intimacy can return, and when it does, it can be even deeper than before.

If you're a man reading this and you've struggled with your sex drive, your desires—I want you to know you're not alone. You're not broken. You're not failing. You're learning. You're growing. You're becoming.

You don't have to be perfect. You don't have to be fearless. You just have to be honest.

Chapter Twelve

INFIDELITY

Infidelity is one of the most painful and complex struggles a man can face—whether he's the one who strays or the one betrayed. It's not just about sex. It's about identity, unmet needs, emotional disconnection, and sometimes, deep confusion about what it means to love and be loved.

For many men, infidelity isn't about conquest—it's about escape. It's about trying to fill a void they don't know how to name. Sometimes it's loneliness. Sometimes it's resentment. Sometimes it's the fear of aging, of fading, of being invisible. Sometimes it's the need to feel desired, admired, chosen. And when those needs aren't met—or when they're buried under years of silence and stress—men look elsewhere. Not always consciously. Not always maliciously. But destructively, nonetheless.

There's also the pressure of performance. Men are often taught that their worth is tied to their virility, their desirability, their ability to attract. And when life gets hard—when marriage feels routine, when intimacy fades, when communication breaks down—that pressure doesn't go away. It just finds new outlets. Affairs can feel like a shortcut to validation. A way to feel alive again. But it's a lie. A temporary fix that leaves deeper wounds.

I've seen men stray from their marriages not because they stopped loving their spouses, but because they felt lost in how to express what was missing. It wasn't a lack of love — it was a lack of language. They didn't know how to say, "I feel unwanted," or "I'm struggling with the tension between us." They didn't know how to talk about the constant battles over intimacy, the exhaustion of feeling rejected or pressured, or the quiet ache of emotional and physical disconnect.

Some felt unseen — not just sexually, but emotionally. Their spouse had stopped caring for themselves, and in turn, they felt forgotten. The spark that once lit up their relationship had dimmed, and they didn't know how to reignite it. They didn't know how to ask for desire, for attention, for tenderness. They didn't know how to say, "I miss us."

And when the silence grew louder than the love, when the distance felt unbearable, they didn't seek resolution — they sought relief. Not because they wanted to betray their vows, but because they didn't know how to repair what had broken. They didn't know how to name their pain, so they numbed it. They didn't know how to fight for connection, so they escaped the disconnection.

It's not an excuse. It's a tragedy. Because beneath every act of infidelity is often a story of unmet needs, unspoken wounds, and unresolved longing. Healing begins not with blame, but with understanding. With learning to speak the truth before it turns into silence. With learning to ask for help before the heart goes looking elsewhere.

And then there's shame. The kind that builds over time. The kind that tells a man he's failing, that he's not enough, that he's trapped. Shame doesn't lead to healing—it leads to hiding. And hiding is fertile ground for infidelity. Because when you're disconnected from yourself, it's easy to disconnect from your values.

None of this are excuses for betrayal in a marriage. But it helps explain it. It helps us understand the emotional landscape that leads a man to cross a line he swore he never would.

Healing from infidelity—whether you've committed it or been hurt by it—requires brutal honesty. It requires facing the pain, the patterns, the unmet needs. It requires rebuilding trust, not just with others, but with yourself. And it requires learning how to love in a way that's rooted in truth, not fantasy.

Infidelity is one of the most painful breaches of trust a relationship can endure. It cuts deep, not just into the heart of a marriage, but into the soul of the individuals involved. The Bible speaks clearly and consistently about the seriousness of infidelity — not to shame, but to protect. Not to condemn, but to call us back to the sacredness of covenant love.

From the earliest pages of Scripture, we see that marriage is designed to reflect God's faithfulness. In Genesis, when God brings Adam and Eve together, He establishes a bond of unity — "bone of my bones and flesh of my flesh." This union is not just physical; it's spiritual. It's a covenant. And within that covenant, faithfulness is not optional — it's essential.

Throughout the Old Testament, infidelity is treated not only as a personal betrayal but as a spiritual one. In the Ten Commandments, God says plainly: "You shall not commit adultery" (Exodus 20:14). This command isn't just about behaviour — it's about honouring the sacred trust between two people and the God who joined them together.

The book of Proverbs speaks with raw honesty about the consequences of infidelity. It warns of the emotional devastation, the loss of integrity, and the ripple effects that reach far beyond the moment of betrayal. Proverbs 6:32 says, "He who commits adultery lacks sense; he who does it destroys himself." These are not words of judgment — they are words of sorrow. Because adultery doesn't just break a vow; it breaks hearts.

In the New Testament, Jesus deepens the conversation. In Matthew 5:27–28, He teaches that infidelity begins not with the act, but with the intention — with the gaze, the thought, the desire. He's not raising the bar to make us feel guilty; He's revealing how sacred intimacy truly is. It's not just about what we do — it's about what we nurture in our hearts.

But the Bible doesn't stop at warning. It also offers hope.

In John 8, we meet a woman caught in adultery. The crowd wants to stone her. Jesus kneels beside her. He doesn't excuse her actions, but He also doesn't condemn her. He says, "Neither do I condemn you. Go, and sin no more." In that moment, we see the heart of God — a heart that longs to restore, not reject. A heart that sees the brokenness behind the betrayal and offers grace.

Adultery is serious. It wounds deeply. But it is not beyond redemption. The Bible invites us to take sin seriously — and to take grace even more seriously. For those who have been betrayed, Scripture offers comfort and healing. For those who have strayed, it offers forgiveness and a path back to integrity.

Faithfulness is not just about staying physically loyal. It's about guarding our hearts, honouring our promises, and reflecting the love of a God who never gives up on us. Whether you're healing from betrayal, rebuilding trust, or seeking to protect your marriage, the Bible's message is clear: love is worth fighting for, and grace is always within reach.

If you're a man who's struggled with infidelity, I want you to know you're not beyond redemption. You're not beyond repair. But you must choose honesty. You must choose growth. You must choose love—not the fleeting kind, but the kind that stays.

CHAPTER TWELVE : INFIDELITY

Chapter Thirteen

SEXUAL ADDICTION

Sexual addiction is one of those struggles that many men and women face silently—wrapped in shame, secrecy, and confusion. It's not just about desire. It's about compulsion. About using sex to soothe pain, escape reality, or feel a fleeting sense of control.

Sexual addiction isn't about lust alone. It's about emotional wounds that haven't healed. It's about unmet needs—intimacy, affirmation, safety—that get rerouted into compulsive behaviour. It's about the brain learning to associate pleasure with escape, and then craving that escape more and more.

For many men, it starts early. Exposure to pornography, lack of emotional guidance, cultural messages that equate manhood with sexual conquest. Over time, sex becomes a coping mechanism. A way to manage anxiety, depression, rejection. But it's a short-term fix with long-term consequences.

Recovery isn't about suppressing desire. It's about reclaiming it. It's about learning to feel without numbing. To connect without escaping. To love without performing. It's about building a new relationship with your body, your emotions, your story.

I've talked with other men who've walked this road. Men who felt trapped. Men who felt broken. Men who thought they were the only ones. And every time we talk, there's healing. Because the silence breaks. Because the shame lifts. Because the truth comes out.

Sexual addiction is not a moral failure. It's a human struggle. And it can be healed.

Porn addiction is one of the most widespread and least talked about struggles men face. It's easy to access, socially normalized, and often dismissed as harmless. But the truth is, it rewires the brain. It reshapes desire. It distorts intimacy. And over time, it can leave a man feeling more alone than ever.

Addiction isn't always loud. It doesn't always look like rock bottom. Sometimes it looks like routine. Like habits we don't question. Like patterns we call "normal" because they've been with us so long. For me, addiction crept in quietly. It didn't announce itself. It didn't come with flashing lights or dramatic consequences. It came with comfort. With relief. With the promise of escape.

I've read the research. I've listened to the stories. And I've seen the consequences. Erectile dysfunction in young men is rising—not because of physical issues, but because of psychological ones. When the brain becomes conditioned to artificial stimulation, real-life intimacy can feel dull, awkward, even anxiety-inducing. The dopamine spikes from porn are intense and immediate. Real sex, with all its emotional layers and imperfections, can't compete. And so, the cycle begins: more porn, less connection. More escape, less presence.

Porn doesn't just affect the body—it affects the psyche. It creates unrealistic expectations. It teaches men to associate arousal with novelty, with control, with fantasy. And when those expectations aren't met in real relationships, frustration sets in. Disappointment. Disconnection. Sometimes even resentment.

I've seen marriages fall apart because of porn. Not just because of the secrecy, but because of the emotional withdrawal. A man becomes less engaged, less affectionate, less interested in his partner. He's still sexually active—but not with her. And that kind of betrayal cuts deep. It's not just about sex. It's about intimacy. About trust. About being chosen.

Porn also opens the door to experimentation that often leads to confusion and chaos. I've seen men dabble in open relationships, casual hookups, even risky behaviour—all in search of something they can't quite name. And most of the time, it doesn't end well. Because what they're chasing isn't just pleasure—it's connection. And porn can't give that. It can mimic it. It can simulate it. But it can't sustain it.

The sex industry is massive. Multi-billion-dollar massive. It includes everything from prostitution to human trafficking, sex toys to virtual reality, and it thrives on disconnection. It sells the illusion of intimacy without the vulnerability. And while I believe in freedom of choice, I also believe in truth. And the truth is, many men are being shaped by an industry that doesn't care about their wholeness—only their consumption.

I've had conversations with men who feel trapped. They don't want to keep watching, but they don't know how to stop. They feel ashamed, isolated, confused. And the shame only deepens the addiction. Because when you feel unworthy, you seek escape. And when you escape, you feel more unworthy.

It starts with conversation. Honest, open, courageous conversation between husbands and wives. We need to talk about sex—not just the mechanics, but the meaning. The emotional, spiritual, relational layers. We need to talk about desire—not just what we want, but why we want it. We need to talk about satisfaction—not just what feels good, but what feels whole.

Sexual satisfaction in a relationship isn't automatic. It takes work. It takes communication. It takes vulnerability. It takes the willingness to say, "This is what I need," and the courage to ask, "What do you need?" It's not about performance—it's about presence. It's not about fantasy—it's about connection.

When men and women begin to talk openly about sex, something powerful happens. The shame lifts. The pressure eases. The intimacy deepens. And suddenly, sex becomes not just an act—but a language. A way of saying, "I see you. I choose you. I'm with you."

I've come to believe that porn addiction is one of the most misunderstood and underestimated forces shaping modern masculinity. It's not just about lust. It's about loneliness. It's about emotional disconnection. It's about a generation of men—young and old—who are trying to feel something real in a world that keeps offering them something fake.

I've sat with men in their twenties who are terrified because they can't get aroused with their spouse. They're healthy, they're in love, they want to connect—but their bodies won't respond. And they're ashamed. They think something's wrong with them. They think they're broken. But they're not. Their brains have simply been rewired by years of artificial stimulation. By endless novelty. By dopamine spikes that no real-life moment can match.

And I've talked to men in their sixties who've watched their marriages slowly unravel—not because they stopped loving their wives, but because they stopped showing up. Porn became easier. Less complicated. More predictable. And over time, they stopped pursuing their spouse. Stopped initiating. Stopped engaging. And the emotional distance grew until it became a canyon.

Porn doesn't just affect the bedroom. It affects the heart. It affects the way a man sees women. The way he sees himself. The way he defines intimacy. It teaches him that sex is about control, about performance, about consumption. And when that becomes the lens through which he views relationships, real connection becomes difficult—sometimes impossible.

I've seen how porn addiction opens the door to other struggles. To infidelity. To emotional detachment. To risky behaviour. To open relationships that promise freedom but often deliver confusion and pain. I've seen men chase novelty until they lose sight of what they truly need: safety, intimacy, love.

And I've seen how this addiction is fed by an industry that thrives on exploitation. The sex industry is massive—billions of dollars flowing through pornography, prostitution, trafficking, sex toys, and more. And behind the glossy images and seductive videos are real people. Many of them hurting. Many of them trapped. Many of them used.

Porn addiction isn't just a personal issue—it's a cultural one. It's shaping how men relate to women. How they relate to themselves. How they define masculinity. And it's leaving a trail of broken relationships, fractured identities, and emotional numbness.

But there's hope.

I believe healing begins with honesty. With men being brave enough to say, "I'm struggling." With couples being vulnerable enough to ask, "How can we reconnect?" With communities being safe enough to say, "You're not alone."

I've learned that sexual satisfaction in a marriage isn't automatic. It's intentional. It requires communication. It requires empathy. It requires the willingness to grow together, to learn each other's rhythms, to honour each other's needs. It's not about fantasy—it's about presence. It's not about performance—it's about connection.

When men and women begin to talk openly about sex, something shifts. The shame lifts. The pressure eases. The intimacy deepens. And suddenly, sex becomes not just an act—but a language. A way of saying, "I see you. I choose you. I'm with you."

I've also learned that when sexual needs go unmet—when there's no space for honest conversation—men and women begin to drift. They begin to seek satisfaction elsewhere. Sometimes through infidelity. Sometimes through fantasy. Sometimes through same-sex experiences, masturbation, or artificial stimulation. Not because they're truly fulfilled by it, but because they're searching. Searching for relief. For validation. For something real.

And that's why this conversation matters. Because behind every addiction is a person longing to be whole. To be known. To be loved.

Addiction is a complex and deeply personal struggle that touches every part of a person's life. It's not simply a bad habit or a moral failing—it's a condition that affects the brain, distorts emotions, and often leaves individuals feeling trapped in cycles they don't fully understand. At its core, addiction is a compulsive pursuit of a substance or behaviour despite harmful consequences. Whether it's drugs, alcohol, gambling, pornography, food, or even relationships, addiction often begins as a way to cope with pain, stress, or emptiness. What starts as relief can quickly become dependence, and what once felt like a choice begins to feel like a necessity.

The brain plays a central role in addiction. It's wired to seek pleasure and avoid pain, and when we experience something enjoyable, it releases dopamine—a chemical that reinforces that experience. Addictive substances and behaviours flood the brain with dopamine in unnatural amounts, creating a powerful imprint. Over time, the brain adapts by reducing its sensitivity to dopamine, which means the person needs more of the substance or behaviour to feel the same effect. This rewiring affects the brain's reward system and impairs the prefrontal cortex, which is responsible for decision-making, impulse control, and judgment. As a result, people struggling with addiction often find it difficult to resist urges, even when they know the consequences.

Emotionally, addiction can be devastating. It often leads to shame, isolation, and a deep sense of failure. People may feel disconnected from themselves and others, unable to explain why they continue to do something that hurts them and those they love. Relationships suffer, trust erodes, and self-worth diminishes. The emotional toll is compounded by the secrecy and guilt that often accompany addiction. Many live with a constant inner conflict—wanting to stop but feeling powerless to do so. Depression and anxiety frequently coexist with addiction, creating a cycle that's hard to break.

Despite its grip, addiction is not beyond healing. The brain can recover, emotions can be restored, and lives can be rebuilt. Recovery begins with honesty—acknowledging the struggle and seeking help. It may involve therapy, support groups, medical treatment, spiritual guidance, or a combination of these. Healing is not just about quitting a substance or behaviour; it's about rediscovering joy, rebuilding identity, and learning new ways to cope with life's challenges. It's about replacing isolation with connection and shame with grace.

CHAPTER THIRTEEN : SEXUAL ADDICTION

Chapter Fourteen

ONANISM

Onanism, often referred to as masturbation, is one of the most quietly wrestled struggles among men. It's rarely spoken about openly, yet it touches the lives of many—sometimes with confusion, sometimes with guilt, and often with deep questions about desire, discipline, and spiritual integrity. For some, it begins in adolescence as a natural curiosity about the body. For others, it becomes a coping mechanism for loneliness, stress, or emotional pain. Over time, what may have started as a moment of release can evolve into a habit that feels difficult to control.

Scientifically, masturbation is tied to the brain's reward system. When a man engages in sexual stimulation, the brain releases dopamine and other feel-good chemicals that create a sense of pleasure and relief. This neurological response reinforces the behaviour, making it something the brain begins to crave—not just for physical satisfaction, but for emotional comfort. In moments of anxiety, boredom, or sadness, the brain remembers that this act brought relief, and so it seeks it again.

This cycle can become deeply ingrained, especially when paired with visual stimulation or fantasy, which further intensifies the neurological imprint.

Desire itself is not wrong. It's part of being human. God created us with bodies that respond to touch, with minds that imagine, and with hearts that long for connection. But desire, when left unchecked or misdirected, can lead us away from intimacy and toward isolation. Onanism often becomes a substitute for real connection—a way to feel something without the vulnerability of relationship. It can also become a way to escape emotional discomfort, rather than face it. Over time, this can dull a man's capacity for emotional depth, relational presence, and spiritual clarity.

The Bible doesn't speak directly about masturbation, but it does speak clearly about sexual purity, self-control, and the stewardship of our bodies. The term "onanism" comes from the story of Onan in Genesis 38, who spilled his seed on the ground to avoid fulfilling his duty to provide offspring for his deceased brother's wife. While the context of that story is about disobedience and selfishness, it has historically been linked to the act of masturbation. More broadly, Scripture calls believers to honour God with their bodies, to flee from sexual immorality, and to pursue holiness in thought and action. Jesus, in Matthew 5, speaks of lust as something that begins in the heart, reminding us that purity is not just about what we do, but what we dwell on internally.

Dealing with onanism is not about shame—it's about understanding, healing, and growth. For many men, the struggle is not just physical but emotional and spiritual. It requires honesty, accountability, and often support from trusted mentors, counselors, or faith communities. It may involve identifying triggers, replacing the habit with healthier coping strategies, and learning to sit with discomfort rather than escape it. Prayer, Scripture, and spiritual disciplines can help reorient the heart and mind toward wholeness. The goal is not just to stop a behaviour, but to cultivate a life of integrity, connection, and peace.

Ultimately, the silent struggle of onanism is not beyond redemption. God is not surprised by our battles, nor is He distant from our pain. He meets us in our weakness, not with condemnation, but with grace. The journey toward freedom is not about perfection—it's about progress. It's about learning to live with open hands, honest hearts, and a renewed desire to honour the One who made us, body and soul.

There's a quiet struggle many men face, one that rarely gets talked about in public or even among close friends. It's the addiction to onanism—compulsive masturbation. For some, it begins as a natural part of adolescence, a way to explore the body and understand desire. But for others, it becomes something more. Something that slowly takes over. Something that begins to shape how they relate to themselves, to others, and to intimacy itself.

I've seen how this addiction can take root in the absence of real connection. When sex in a relationship is strained, infrequent, or emotionally disconnected, many men turn inward. They seek release not just from physical tension, but from emotional stress, loneliness, and even boredom. Onanism becomes a way to cope. A way to feel something. A way to escape. And when it's paired with pornography, the cycle deepens. The brain begins to associate arousal with fantasy, with control, with instant gratification. Real intimacy—with its vulnerability, unpredictability, and emotional depth—starts to feel foreign.

In Matthew 5:28, Jesus says, "Anyone who looks at a woman lustfully has already committed adultery with her in his heart." This isn't a condemnation of desire—it's a call to honour it. To steward it. To recognize that sex is sacred, not something to be consumed or exploited. In 1 Thessalonians 4:3–5, Paul urges believers to avoid sexual immorality and to learn to control their bodies in ways that are holy and honourable. These verses remind us that our sex isn't just physical—it's spiritual. It's relational. It's meant to be expressed in love, not isolation.

Addiction to onanism often thrives in secrecy. Men feel ashamed. They feel weak. They feel like they're failing. And so they hide. But hiding only deepens the wound. The more we isolate, the more we depend on the very thing that's hurting us. Healing begins with honesty. With courage. With the willingness to say, "I'm struggling." And with the belief that change is possible.

I believe that men and women need to have open conversations about sex. About desire. About satisfaction. When couples don't talk about their sexual needs, they drift. Emotional and physical intimacy suffer. And in that silence, temptation grows. Infidelity, emotional withdrawal, and even same-sex experimentation or artificial stimulation often begin with unmet needs and unspoken pain. But when there's space for honesty, empathy, and mutual care, couples can build a sexual relationship that's not just satisfying—but sacred.

Sex isn't just about pleasure. It's about connection. About trust. About being fully known and fully accepted. And when that kind of intimacy is cultivated, the need to escape through compulsive behaviour begins to fade. The desire for fantasy is replaced by the joy of presence. The addiction loses its grip.

Temptation is a universal experience, and Scripture acknowledges this. In 1 Corinthians 10:13, Paul writes, "No temptation has overtaken you except what is common to mankind. And God is faithful; he will not let you be tempted beyond what you can bear. But when you are tempted, he will also provide a way out so that you can endure it." This verse offers hope. It reminds us that we're not alone in our struggles, and that God provides strength and escape when we seek Him.

Ultimately, the Bible calls men to live with purity, self-control, and love. Galatians 5:16 says, "So I say, walk by the Spirit, and you will not gratify the desires of the flesh." This isn't a call to perfection—it's a call to transformation. To live not by impulse, but by intention. To seek connection over consumption. To pursue intimacy over isolation.

If you're a man wrestling with this struggle, know that you're not alone. The path to healing begins with honesty—with yourself, with God, and with those you trust. Masturbation may offer temporary relief, but it cannot replace the depth of real intimacy, emotional connection, and spiritual peace. And that's something every man should know.

CHAPTER FOURTEEN : ONANISM

Chapter Fifteen

DISCIPLINE AND SELF-CARE

There's a quiet neglect that many men live with. It doesn't show up in dramatic ways—not at first. It shows up in fatigue, in irritability, in the slow erosion of joy. It shows up in the way we stop looking in the mirror, stop caring how we feel, stop checking in with ourselves. We become husbands, fathers, brothers, friends, colleagues—roles we carry with pride. But somewhere along the way, we forget to be someone to ourselves.

I've seen this pattern in my own life. Seasons where I was so focused on showing up for others that I stopped showing up for me. I'd make sure everyone else was fed, supported, encouraged—but I was running on fumes. I'd say yes to every request, every responsibility, every need—except my own. And eventually, it caught up with me. Not in a breakdown, but in a slow unraveling. I felt disconnected from my body, from my emotions, from my sense of self.

Self-care isn't selfish. It's stewardship. Just as we tend to our spiritual lives—through prayer, reflection, worship—we must tend to our physical and emotional lives. The body is not just a vessel; it's a voice. It tells us when we're tired, when we're stressed, when we're out of alignment. And if we ignore it long enough, it stops whispering and starts shouting.

I've learned that how I carry myself matters. How I look, how I smell, how I walk—these aren't superficial details. They're reflections of how I feel inside. When I take time to groom myself, to dress with intention, to move with confidence, I'm not just presenting myself to the world—I'm reminding myself that I matter. That I'm worth the effort.

There was a time when I thought self-care was indulgent. Spas, massages, hobbies, gym memberships—those were luxuries, not necessities. But I was wrong. I remember the first time I went to a spa. I felt awkward, out of place. But as I sat in silence, as my body relaxed, as my mind slowed down, I realized something: I hadn't felt that kind of peace in months. Maybe years. And I wondered why I had waited so long to give myself permission to rest.

Exercise became another form of self-care for me. Not just for fitness, but for clarity. For emotional release. For reclaiming my energy. I started walking more, lifting weights, stretching. And with each movement, I felt more connected to myself. More grounded. More alive.

Hobbies, too, became sacred. I picked up woodworking for a while. Then photography. Then journaling. None of them were about achievement—they were about presence. About doing something that fed my soul. About creating space where I wasn't performing, but simply being.

Self-care also means emotional honesty. Checking in with myself. Asking, "How am I really doing?" It means saying no when I need to.

It means setting boundaries. It means allowing myself to feel without judgment. To cry if I need to. To rest if I need to. To be human.

I've seen too many men burn out because they believed they had to be everything to everyone. They carried the weight of the world but never paused to care for the man beneath the armor. And when they finally collapsed, they didn't know how to rebuild—because they had never learned how to nurture themselves.

Self-care is a discipline. It's a practice. It's a commitment to wholeness. And it doesn't require perfection—it requires intention. A few minutes of silence. A walk in the park. A good meal. A deep breath. A conversation with someone who sees you. These moments add up. They restore. They heal.

There's a quiet kind of exhaustion that creeps into a man's life when he's spent too long taking care of everyone but himself. I've seen it in fathers who give everything to their children, husbands who pour themselves into their marriages, leaders who carry the weight of their communities, and friends who are always available but rarely honest about their own needs. Somewhere along the way, we confuse selflessness with self-neglect. We forget that we are not machines—we are men. And men need care, too.

The Bible speaks to this more than we realize. In Psalm 139:14, David writes, "I praise you because I am fearfully and wonderfully made; your works are wonderful, I know that full well." That verse isn't just poetic—it's foundational. You were made with intention. You are not an accident. And when you care for yourself, you honour the One who created you.

In 1 Corinthians 6:19–20, Paul reminds us, "Do you not know that your bodies are temples of the Holy Spirit… You are not your own; you were bought at a price. Therefore, honour God with your bodies." That's not just a call to purity—it's a call to care. To treat your body with reverence. To nourish it, rest it, strengthen it. To see it as sacred, not secondary.

Even Jesus practiced self-care. In Luke 5:16, we read, "But Jesus often withdrew to lonely places and prayed." He didn't wait until He was burned out—He made space for solitude, for rest, for renewal. If the Son of God needed time to recharge, how much more do we?

In Matthew 11:28, Jesus offers one of the most tender invitations in all of Scripture: "Come to me, all you who are weary and burdened, and I will give you rest." That's not just spiritual rest—it's holistic. It's emotional, physical, relational. It's the kind of rest that restores your soul and resets your body.

I've learned that self-care also means investing in yourself. Picking up a hobby. Reading a book. Taking a class. Going to therapy. Saying no when you need to. Saying yes to joy. It means going to the spa if that helps you unwind. It means taking a walk without your phone. It means creating space in your life that isn't filled with obligation, but with intention.

Too many men live as if their worth is measured by how much they give. But your worth is not in your output—it's in your being. You are valuable, even when you're resting. You are loved, even when you're not producing. You are worthy of care, even when no one else is asking for it.

Self-care is more than bubble baths and quiet evenings. It's a holistic practice that touches every part of our lives—body, mind, heart, and soul. When we care for ourselves intentionally, we create space for healing, growth, and resilience. We become more present, more grounded, and more capable of showing up for others. And it's best understood through eight interconnected areas that together form a foundation for well-being.

Physical self-care is often the most visible. It includes the basics—nutrition, movement, and rest. Eating nourishing foods fuels the body and stabilizes mood. Exercise strengthens muscles, boosts energy, and releases endorphins that help combat stress. Sleep is the quiet healer, restoring the body and mind each night. Physical care also includes hydration, regular checkups, and listening to the body's signals. When we treat our bodies with kindness, we build a home for our spirit to thrive.

Mental self-care is about tending to our thoughts. It involves practices like mindfulness, which teaches us to observe without judgment. Positive self-talk helps reframe inner narratives that may be rooted in fear or shame. Therapy offers a safe space to unpack patterns and gain clarity. Mental care also includes setting boundaries with technology, engaging in creative expression, and giving ourselves permission to rest from constant productivity. A healthy mind is not one that never struggles, but one that knows how to return to peace.

Emotional self-care invites us to feel deeply and honestly. It means acknowledging our emotions without being overwhelmed by them. Gratitude helps shift our focus from lack to abundance. Managing triggers requires awareness and compassion, not avoidance. Journaling allows us to process experiences and reflect on growth. Emotional care also includes crying when we need to, laughing freely, and seeking comfort in safe relationships. When we honour our emotions, we learn to live with authenticity.

Spiritual self-care connects us to something greater than ourselves. It may involve prayer, meditation, or time in nature. Forest bathing—simply being among trees—can calm the nervous system and awaken awe. Yoga blends movement and breath, grounding us in the present. Spiritual care isn't about rigid rituals; it's about finding meaning, purpose, and connection. Whether through silence, scripture, or song, tending to the spirit brings depth to our days.

Intellectual self-care feeds the mind's curiosity. Reading opens new worlds and perspectives. Learning a new skill or exploring a hobby keeps the brain engaged and inspired. Intellectual care also includes critical thinking, open dialogue, and creative problem-solving. It's not about being perfect or productive—it's about staying mentally alive. When we challenge ourselves to grow, we expand our capacity to understand and contribute.

Environmental self-care is often overlooked, but it matters deeply. Our surroundings affect our mood, energy, and sense of safety. A clean space can bring clarity; a cluttered one can breed stress. Creating a home that feels peaceful, organizing our workspace, or adding beauty through plants or art can uplift the spirit. Environmental care also includes protecting ourselves from toxic influences, whether physical or emotional. When our space supports us, we feel more at ease.

Social self-care is about connection. It means nurturing relationships that are life-giving and setting boundaries with those that drain us. It includes knowing our limitations, communicating needs, and making time for meaningful interactions. Social care also involves solitude—choosing quiet when we need it. True connection doesn't come from constant contact, but from intentional presence. When we feel seen and supported, we flourish.

Financial self-care brings stability and peace of mind. It includes budgeting, saving, and making informed decisions. It's not about wealth—it's about wisdom. Financial care also means addressing money-related stress, setting goals, and seeking help when needed. When we manage our resources with intention, we reduce anxiety and create freedom. Money may not buy happiness, but financial clarity can open doors to a more balanced life.

Each area of self-care is a thread in the tapestry of well-being. When we weave them together, we create a life that is not just functional, but fulfilling. Self-care is not a checklist—it's a rhythm. It's the gentle art of returning to ourselves, again and again, with compassion and grace.

Chapter Sixteen

GODLY CHARACTER

There's something deeply powerful about a man who walks in godly character. Not because he's perfect, but because he's consistent. Because he's anchored. Because he's the same man in private as he is in public. I've always admired men like that—men whose lives speak louder than their words. Men who carry integrity, kindness, and humility like second skin. And I've tried, imperfectly, to become one of them.

Godly character isn't built overnight. It's shaped in the quiet places. In the decisions no one sees. In the moments when compromise would be easier, but conviction wins out. I remember a time early in my career when I was offered a shortcut—an opportunity to gain influence by bending the truth. It wasn't illegal. It wasn't even dramatic. But it didn't sit right with me. I wrestled with it for days. And in the end, I chose the harder path. I lost the opportunity, but I kept my peace. And that peace was worth more than any promotion.

Integrity is the foundation of godly character. Proverbs 10:9 says, "Whoever walks in integrity walks securely, but whoever takes crooked paths will be found out." That verse has stayed with me. Integrity isn't just about honesty—it's about wholeness. About being undivided. About living in a way that doesn't require hiding.

Proverbs 11:3 says, "The integrity of the upright guides them, but the unfaithful are destroyed by their duplicity." I've seen men lose everything—marriages, careers, friendships—because they compromised their integrity. And I've seen men walk through fire and come out stronger because they refused to.

Kindness is another pillar. In a world that often rewards aggression and dominance, kindness can feel like weakness. But it's not. It's strength under control. It's choosing gentleness when you could choose power. Galatians 5:22–23 lists kindness as one of the fruits of the Spirit: "But the fruit of the Spirit is love, joy, peace, patience, kindness, goodness, faithfulness, gentleness and self-control." These aren't just traits—they're evidence. Evidence that the Spirit is at work in a man's life.

We're taught to be tough, to be efficient, to be in control. But kindness requires softness. It requires empathy. It requires slowing down long enough to see someone else's pain. I've had moments where a simple act of kindness—holding a door, offering a compliment, listening without interrupting—opened the door to deeper connection. And I've had moments where my lack of kindness closed that door.

I've had moments when kindness changed everything. A tense meeting. A difficult conversation. A moment of conflict. And instead of reacting, I paused. I listened. I responded with grace. And the atmosphere shifted. Not because I was clever, but because I was kind. Kindness disarms. It heals. It builds bridges.

The gifts of the Spirit are equally important. They're not earned—they're given. But they're meant to be used with character. 1 Corinthians 12 speaks of gifts like wisdom, knowledge, faith, healing, prophecy, and discernment. These gifts are powerful. But without love, they're empty. That's why Paul writes in 1 Corinthians 13:2, "If I have the gift of prophecy and can fathom all mysteries and all knowledge... but do not have love, I am nothing." Character is what gives gifts their weight. Their credibility. Their impact.

I've seen men with incredible gifts lose their influence because they lacked character. And I've seen men with quiet gifts change lives because they walked in humility, integrity, and love. The difference wasn't talent—it was trustworthiness.

Godly character also means being teachable. Proverbs 12:1 says, "Whoever loves discipline loves knowledge, but whoever hates correction is stupid." That's blunt—but true. I've had to learn how to receive correction. How to admit when I'm wrong. How to grow. And every time I've humbled myself, I've grown stronger—not weaker.

It means being faithful. In your marriage. In your friendships. In your commitments. Luke 16:10 says, "Whoever can be trusted with very little can also be trusted with much." Faithfulness in the small things builds the foundation for the big things.

It means walking in love. Not just romantic love, but sacrificial love. The kind that shows up. That forgives. That stays. Ephesians 5:2 says, "And walk in love, as Christ loved us and gave himself up for us." That's the standard. Not convenience—but sacrifice.

Building godly character is a lifelong journey. It's not about perfection—it's about direction. It's about choosing, day by day, to reflect the heart of God. To be a man who can be trusted. Who loves deeply. Who serves humbly. Who leads with grace.

If you're a man reading this and you feel like you've fallen short, I want you to know: you're not alone. We all have. But character isn't about never falling—it's about getting back up. About choosing integrity over image. Kindness over ego. Love over pride.

Building godly character is one of the most important—and most difficult—journeys a man can take. It's not about being flawless. It's about being faithful. It's about choosing integrity when no one's watching, choosing kindness when it's inconvenient, and choosing humility when pride would be easier. I've learned that godly character isn't built in the spotlight—it's forged in the quiet, daily decisions that shape who we are.

Most men I know want to be good. They want to be honest, dependable, loving. But life has a way of testing those intentions. Stress, disappointment, temptation, and pressure all chip away at our resolve. I've seen men lose their temper with their kids, lie to protect their reputation, cheat to get ahead, or withdraw emotionally from their families—not because they're evil, but because they're tired. Because they're overwhelmed. Because they're human.

I remember a friend who was known for his generosity and leadership in our community. He was the kind of guy people looked up to. But behind closed doors, he was struggling. His marriage was strained, his finances were tight, and he felt like he was failing as a father. One day, he confessed to me that he had started cutting corners at work—justifying it as survival. "I'm not proud of it," he said, "but I feel like I'm drowning." That moment stuck with me. Because it reminded me that godly character isn't just about doing the right thing—it's about having the courage to admit when you're not.

The Bible gives us a clear picture of what godly character looks like. Galatians 5:22–23 lists the fruit of the Spirit: "love, joy, peace, patience, kindness, goodness, faithfulness, gentleness, and self-control." These aren't just virtues—they're evidence. They show up in how we treat our spouse when we're frustrated. In how we respond to criticism. In how we handle money, power, and influence.

But let's be honest—these qualities don't come naturally. Most men struggle with patience. We want results. We want control. We want respect. And when we don't get it, we react. We raise our voice. We shut down. We isolate. That's why self-control is so critical. Proverbs 16:32 says, "Better a patient man than a warrior, one with self-control than one who takes a city." That verse flips the script. It tells us that true strength isn't about dominance—it's about discipline.

One of the most common struggles men face is compartmentalization. We act one way at church, another way at work, and another way at home. We wear masks to fit the moment. But godly character calls us to be whole. To be the same man in every room. That's hard. It requires courage. It requires consistency. It requires grace.

I've also learned that building godly character means being teachable. Proverbs 27:17 says, "As iron sharpens iron, so one man sharpens another." We need other men. We need accountability. We need mentors. We need brothers who will call us out, lift us up, and remind us who we are when we forget.

And we need to be honest with God. Psalm 139:23–24 says, "Search me, God, and know my heart; test me and know my anxious thoughts. See if there is any offensive way in me, and lead me in the way everlasting." That's a dangerous prayer—but a necessary one. Because godly character isn't about behaviour modification. It's about heart transformation.

If you're a man reading this and you feel like you're falling short, I want you to know: you're not alone. We all struggle. We all stumble. But the goal isn't perfection—it's progress. It's choosing to grow. To repent. To forgive. To try again.

Godly character isn't built in a day. It's built in the daily. In the quiet choices. In the hard conversations. In the moments when no one's watching.

Chapter Seventeen

A BLUEPRINT

Every man, whether he realizes it or not, is building something with his life. Some build careers. Some build families. Some build reputations. But the question that haunts me—and many men I've walked with—is this: What am I leaving behind? What will outlive me? What kind of blueprint am I creating for those who come after?

Legacy isn't just about wealth or accomplishments. It's about impact. It's about the fingerprints we leave on hearts, not just on paper. I've spent years mentoring younger men, coaching leaders, and walking alongside those trying to find their way. And I've come to believe that legacy begins with intentionality. You don't drift into a meaningful life—you design it.

I remember one young man I mentored during my early years in leadership. He was bright, full of potential, but deeply insecure. He didn't believe he had anything to offer. We met weekly—sometimes over coffee, sometimes in silence. I didn't give him a formula. I gave him presence. I asked questions. I listened. I shared my failures and successes. And slowly, he began to grow. Not because I was brilliant, but because I was available. Years later, he became a mentor himself. That's legacy. That's the blueprint multiplying.

The Bible speaks often about legacy and mentorship. In 2 Timothy 2:2, Paul writes to Timothy, "And the things you have heard me say in the presence of many witnesses entrust to reliable people who will also be qualified to teach others." That's four generations of impact in one verse—Paul to Timothy, Timothy to reliable people, reliable people to others. That's how legacy works. It's not about one man doing everything. It's about one man investing in others who will carry the torch forward.

Proverbs 13:22 says, "A good man leaves an inheritance to his children's children." That inheritance isn't just financial—it's spiritual, emotional, relational. It's wisdom. It's character. It's the kind of life that echoes through generations.

Creating a blueprint means living with vision. It means asking, "What kind of man do I want to be remembered as?" It means writing values into your daily choices. It means showing up when it's inconvenient. It means forgiving when it's hard. It means loving when it's costly.

I've had mentors who shaped me profoundly. Some were older men who spoke truth into my life when I was drifting. Others were peers who challenged me to grow. And some were younger men who reminded me of the fire I once had. Mentorship isn't a one-way street—it's a shared journey. It's iron sharpening iron, as Proverbs 27:17 says: "As iron sharpens iron, so one person sharpens another."

Coaching is part of that blueprint too. It's more structured than mentorship, but just as personal. I've coached men through career transitions, marriage struggles, spiritual dry spells. And every time, I've seen the same truth: men don't need perfect answers—they need honest presence. They need someone to say, "I've been there. You're not alone. Let's walk together."

Legacy also means modeling. You can't teach what you don't live. If I want my son and sons-in-law—or any young man watching me—to be kind, I have to show kindness. If I want them to be men of integrity, I have to tell the truth when it costs me. If I want them to be faithful, I have to stay when it's hard. That's the blueprint. Not just words, but witness.

Psalm 78:4 says, "We will not hide them from their descendants; we will tell the next generation the praiseworthy deeds of the Lord, his power, and the wonders he has done." That's legacy. That's storytelling. That's passing down truth, not just tradition.

I've also learned that legacy isn't built in grand gestures—it's built in daily faithfulness. In showing up for dinner. In praying with your kids. In calling your friend back. In choosing integrity when no one's watching. These small choices stack up. They become the framework of a life that matters.

If you're a man reading this and you feel like you haven't built much yet, I want you to know it's not too late. Legacy isn't about age—it's about intention. You can start today. You can mentor someone. You can coach someone. You can live with vision. You can write a new blueprint.

Because every man leaves something behind. The question is: will it be accidental or intentional? Will it fade or will it multiply?

Every man is building something with his life. Whether he's aware of it or not, his choices, habits, relationships, and values are laying down a blueprint—one that others will follow, inherit, or be shaped by. The question isn't whether you're leaving a legacy. The question is: what kind?

I've spent years mentoring younger men, coaching leaders, and walking alongside those trying to find their way. And I've seen the same struggle again and again: men who want to leave a mark but don't know where to start. They're overwhelmed by the pressure to succeed, unsure of their purpose, and often haunted by the fear that they'll be forgotten. Some are fathers trying to raise sons without having had a father themselves. Some are professionals who've climbed the ladder but feel empty at the top. Some are young men who've never had someone say, "I believe in you."

Legacy isn't about perfection—it's about intention. It's about showing up, being present, and choosing to live a life worth imitating. I remember a man I coached who had built a successful business but felt disconnected from his children. He told me, "I gave them everything except myself." That sentence broke something in me. Because I've felt that tension too—the pull between providing and being present. Between building something and being someone.

Scripture speaks clearly about legacy and mentorship. In 2 Timothy 2:2, Paul writes, "And the things you have heard me say in the presence of many witnesses entrust to reliable people who will also be qualified to teach others." That's legacy in motion—Paul to Timothy, Timothy to others, and those others to the next generation. It's not about one man doing everything. It's about one man investing in others who will carry the torch forward.

Proverbs 13:22 says, "A good man leaves an inheritance to his children's children." That inheritance isn't just financial—it's spiritual, emotional, and relational. It's wisdom passed down through stories, habits, and example. It's the kind of life that echoes through generations.

But building a blueprint isn't easy. Most men struggle with consistency. We start strong, then get distracted. We make promises, then get overwhelmed. We want to mentor others, but feel unqualified. We want to coach, but don't know where to begin. I've had seasons where I felt like I was failing at everything—work, marriage, fatherhood. And in those moments, I questioned whether I had anything worth passing on.

That's when I learned that legacy isn't built in the spotlight—it's built in the shadows. In the quiet decisions. In the daily faithfulness. In the way you treat your spouse when no one's watching. In the way you speak to your children when you're tired. In the way you handle disappointment, temptation, and success.

I've mentored young men who were hungry for guidance but had never been taught how to ask for help. One young man came to me after a church service and said, "I don't know how to be a man. I never had one in my life." We started meeting weekly. I didn't give him lectures— I gave him time. I asked questions. I shared my own failures. And slowly, he began to grow. Not because I was perfect, but because I was present.

Mentorship isn't about having all the answers. It's about walking with someone through the questions. It's about being a safe place. A steady voice. A living example. Proverbs 27:17 says, "As iron sharpens iron, so one man sharpens another." That sharpening doesn't happen through performance—it happens through relationship.

Coaching is about helping someone identify their goals, overcome obstacles, and grow in confidence. I've coached men through career transitions, marriage struggles, spiritual dry spells. And every time, I've seen the same truth: men don't need perfect advice—they need honest presence. They need someone to say, "I've been there. You're not alone. Let's walk together."

One of the biggest barriers to legacy is shame. Many men feel disqualified by their past. They think, "I've messed up too much. I've failed too often. I'm not someone others should follow." But the truth is, your scars can become someone else's roadmap. Your failures can become someone else's wisdom. Your story—no matter how messy—can become someone else's hope.

Psalm 78:4 says, "We will not hide them from their descendants; we will tell the next generation the praiseworthy deeds of the Lord, his power, and the wonders he has done." That's legacy. That's storytelling. That's passing down truth, not just tradition.

Legacy, coaching, and mentoring are not just concepts reserved for boardrooms or biographies. They are lifelines for men seeking to grow, heal, and lead with purpose. In a world that often measures masculinity by performance, power, or silence, these three pillars offer something deeper: transformation. They invite men to become more than what they've inherited, more than what they've survived, and more than what they've been told they should be.

Legacy is what we live out while we're here. It's the values we embody, the choices we make, and the impact we have on those around us. Every man carries a legacy—whether he's aware of it or not. It might be shaped by his father's example, his culture, his faith, or his wounds. But legacy is not fixed. It can be rewritten. A man who chooses integrity over impulse, kindness over control, and presence over performance is crafting a legacy that speaks louder than any title or possession. Legacy asks us: What story are you telling with your life? What will your children, your friends, your community remember about you—not just in words, but in how they felt around you?

Legacy begins with awareness. We must help young men understand the stories they carry—both the ones they've inherited and the ones they're writing. This means encouraging reflection on family values, cultural influences, and personal experiences. It also means challenging destructive patterns and choosing to build something better. Legacy becomes real when we ask, "What kind of man do I want to be?" and "What do I want those who come after me to remember?" In the blueprint, legacy is the foundation—it's the why behind the journey.

Coaching is the art of drawing out potential. It's not about fixing someone—it's about helping them see what's already within. For men, coaching can be a powerful tool to break through stagnation, clarify vision, and build discipline. A good coach doesn't just give advice; he asks the right questions. He listens. He challenges. He holds you accountable to the man you say you want to be. Coaching helps men move from intention to action. It's the bridge between dreaming and doing. Whether it's in fitness, leadership, relationships, or emotional health, coaching offers structure, support, and strategy. It reminds men that growth is not accidental—it's intentional.

Coaching provides the structure. It's the intentional guidance that helps young men set goals, develop discipline, and stay accountable. In the blueprint, coaching shows up through programs, workshops, and one-on-one relationships that focus on skill-building and personal development. It's about teaching emotional intelligence, conflict resolution, financial literacy, and leadership. Coaching helps young men move from potential to purpose. It gives them the tools to navigate life with clarity and confidence.

Mentoring goes deeper. It's relational. It's about walking alongside someone, sharing wisdom, and offering presence. A mentor is someone who's been there—who's failed, learned, and still believes in the journey. For younger men, having a mentor can be life-changing. It provides a safe space to ask hard questions, to be vulnerable, and to receive guidance without judgment. For older men, becoming a mentor is a way to give back, to pour into others what life has taught them. Mentoring is not about perfection—it's about authenticity. It's about saying, "I've walked this road. Let me walk with you." In a culture that often isolates men, mentoring creates connection. It builds bridges between generations. It heals.

Mentoring brings the heart. It's the relational thread that ties generations together. In the blueprint, mentoring is about older men showing up—not as perfect examples, but as honest companions. It's about sharing stories, listening deeply, and offering wisdom without judgment. Mentoring creates safe spaces for vulnerability, questions, and growth. It teaches young men that they don't have to figure it all out alone. It reminds them that strength is found in connection, not isolation.

To develop as men, we need all three. We need to reflect on our legacy—what we've inherited and what we're creating. We need coaching to sharpen our skills, challenge our habits, and push us toward excellence. And we need mentoring to remind us that we're not alone, that wisdom is meant to be shared, and that growth is a communal journey. These aren't luxuries—they're necessities. They help men become more whole, more grounded, and more capable of leading lives that matter.

The world doesn't just need strong men. It needs wise men. Present men. Men who know their story and are willing to help others write theirs. Legacy, coaching, and mentoring are the tools. The transformation is up to us.

To integrate these elements, we need intentional environments— homes, schools, churches, and communities that value character as much as achievement. We need fathers, uncles, coaches, teachers, and elders who are willing to invest time, speak truth, and model integrity. We need rites of passage that mark transitions with meaning, not just age. We need circles of trust where boys become men through shared experience, honest conversation, and spiritual grounding.

The blueprint is not rigid—it's relational. It adapts to culture, context, and personality. But its core remains the same: help young men know who they are, where they're going, and who's walking with them. When legacy, coaching, and mentoring are integrated with intention, we don't just raise men—we raise leaders, protectors, creators, and healers. We raise a generation that knows how to stand tall, speak truth, and live with purpose.

To build a blueprint for the next generation of men, we must intentionally weave together legacy, coaching, and mentoring into the fabric of everyday life. These aren't just abstract ideals—they're practical tools for shaping character, cultivating leadership, and passing down wisdom. When integrated with care and purpose, they become a living framework that helps young men grow into grounded, resilient, and visionary individuals.

Creating a blueprint means living with vision. It means asking, "What kind of man do I want to be remembered as?" It means writing values into your daily choices. It means showing up when it's inconvenient. It means forgiving when it's hard. It means loving when it's costly.

If you're a man reading this and you feel like you haven't built much yet, I want you to know it's not too late. Legacy isn't about age—it's about intention. You can start today. You can mentor someone. You can coach someone. You can live with vision. You can write a new blueprint.

CHAPTER SEVENTEEN : A BLUEPRINT

Chapter Eighteen

STRENGTHS AND WEAKNESSES

The Bible is filled with stories of men—flawed, complex, courageous, broken, redeemed. These weren't superheroes. They were ordinary men who faced temptation, made mistakes, wrestled with doubt, and sometimes failed spectacularly. But what makes their stories powerful is not their perfection—it's their transformation. Their lives mirror the struggles men face today: identity, leadership, failure, temptation, regret, and the longing to leave a legacy.

Adam – The First Man. Adam had everything—a perfect relationship with God, a beautiful wife, and a garden full of abundance. But he made a choice that changed history. He listened to the wrong voice and disobeyed God (Genesis 3). His weakness was passivity. He stood silent when he should have spoken. Many men today struggle with the same thing—avoiding hard conversations, failing to lead in their homes, letting fear or comfort override conviction. Yet even after the fall, God clothed Adam and promised redemption. Mistakes don't end the story—they begin the need for grace.

Adam's failure wasn't just eating the fruit—it was his silence. He stood by while Eve was deceived and didn't intervene. Many men today struggle with passivity. They avoid conflict, stay quiet in their marriages, and let others lead while they disengage. I've spoken with husbands who say, "I just want peace," but their silence creates distance. Adam's story reminds us that leadership requires presence, not just position. And even after failure, God still pursued him.

Noah was righteous in a corrupt generation. He obeyed God when no one else did and built the ark that saved humanity (Genesis 6–9). But after the flood, he got drunk and exposed himself in shame. I've met men who've built successful lives—careers, families, ministries—only to collapse privately under the weight of stress or addiction. One man told me, "I drink to shut off the noise." Noah's story shows that even the faithful need boundaries, rest, and recovery. Obedience doesn't make you immune to burnout.

His strength was obedience; his weakness was self-control. Many men today build great things—businesses, families, ministries—but struggle privately with addiction or emotional collapse. Noah reminds us that even the faithful need boundaries and recovery.

Abraham is called the father of faith, yet he lied twice about his wife to save himself (Genesis 12, 20). He doubted God's promise and slept with Hagar, creating conflict that still echoes today. His strength was vision; his weakness was fear. Like many men, he wanted control when trust was required. But God still fulfilled His promise through Abraham. Legacy isn't built on perfection—it's built on perseverance.

Today, men often feel pressure to control outcomes—financially, relationally, spiritually. I've coached men who manipulate situations out of fear, not malice. Abraham's journey teaches us that faith means trusting God's timing, even when it's uncomfortable. And that mistakes don't cancel the promise.

Moses led Israel out of slavery, parted the Red Sea, and spoke with God face to face. Yet he killed a man in anger, struck the rock instead of speaking to it, and wasn't allowed to enter the Promised Land (Exodus 2, Numbers 20). His strength was leadership; his weakness was emotion. Many men today lead well but struggle with temper, impatience, or burnout. Moses teaches us that calling doesn't erase humanity—but humility can redeem it.

I've met fathers who yell at their kids, professionals who explode under pressure, and men who regret the damage their temper has caused. One man said, "I don't know why I get so angry—it just builds." Moses shows us that leadership requires emotional maturity, and that even great men need healing.

Samson is one of the most fascinating and complex figures in the Bible. His story, found in the book of Judges chapters 13 through 16, is filled with power, passion, and tragedy. Chosen by God before birth to be a Nazirite—a person set apart for divine purposes—Samson was gifted with extraordinary physical strength. His mission was to begin delivering Israel from the oppression of the Philistines, and his strength was a symbol of God's presence and purpose in his life.

Samson's greatest strength was not just his physical power, but the divine calling that rested on him. He was capable of incredible feats: tearing apart a lion with his bare hands, defeating entire battalions of Philistines, and carrying the gates of a city on his shoulders. These acts weren't just displays of brute force—they were signs of God's empowerment. Samson was a man chosen to stand against injustice and to protect his people. His strength was a gift, but it came with a responsibility to live in obedience and humility.

Yet Samson's weaknesses were just as pronounced. He struggled with impulsiveness, pride, and a lack of discernment in relationships. His desire for women—especially those outside of his faith and culture—often led him into dangerous situations. He broke his Nazirite vows, including touching dead bodies and eventually revealing the secret of his strength to Delilah, a woman who betrayed him. Samson's downfall wasn't just physical—it was spiritual. He allowed his desires to override his calling, and in doing so, he lost sight of the source of his strength.

Despite his failures, Samson's story doesn't end in defeat. In his final moments, blinded and imprisoned, he turns back to God. He prays for strength one last time—not for revenge alone, but to fulfill his purpose. And God answers. Samson brings down the temple of the Philistines, sacrificing himself to defeat Israel's enemies. His death becomes a moment of redemption, showing that even in brokenness, God can still use us.

The lessons from Samson's life are profound. Strength without wisdom is dangerous. Calling without character can lead to ruin. But even when we fall, grace is still available. Samson reminds us that our gifts are not enough—we need humility, obedience, and a heart that stays close to God. He teaches us that failure is not final, and that redemption is always possible when we turn back to the One who called us.

David was a man after God's own heart. He wrote psalms, defeated giants, and ruled with courage. But he also committed adultery with Bathsheba and arranged her husband's death (2 Samuel 11). His strength was worship; his weakness was lust. His story is a mirror for men who love God but fall into sexual sin. David's repentance in Psalm 51 shows that brokenness can lead to restoration—and that God values a contrite heart more than a clean record. I've counselled men who've had affairs, struggled with porn, or felt trapped in cycles of lust. One said, "I never thought I'd be that guy." David's repentance in Psalm 51 is raw and real. His story proves that no sin is too great for grace, and that brokenness can lead to deeper intimacy with God.

Solomon asked for wisdom and received it in abundance. He built the temple and wrote Proverbs. But he married foreign women, worshipped false gods, and let his heart drift (1 Kings 11). His strength was discernment; his weakness was compromise. Many men today start strong but lose focus—distracted by success, relationships, or comfort. Solomon reminds us that wisdom must be guarded, not just gained. I've seen men who begin with passion and purpose, only to drift into distraction—chasing success, relationships, or comfort. One man told me, "I used to pray every day. Now I just scroll." Solomon reminds us that wisdom must be guarded, not just gained. Finishing well matters.

Elijah called down fire from heaven and confronted kings. But after one threat from Jezebel, he ran into the wilderness and begged God to take his life (1 Kings 19). His strength was boldness; his weakness was despair. Depression and burnout are real struggles for men today— especially those in leadership. Elijah's story shows that even spiritual giants need rest, renewal, and reassurance. I've sat with pastors, CEOs, and fathers who say, "I'm done. I can't do this anymore." Elijah's story shows that even spiritual giants need rest, renewal, and reassurance. God didn't rebuke him—He fed him, spoke gently, and reminded him he wasn't alone.

Jonah was called to preach to Nineveh but ran in the opposite direction. He was swallowed by a fish, reluctantly obeyed, and then sulked when God showed mercy (Jonah 1–4). His strength was calling; his weakness was pride. Many men today resist God's direction, especially when it challenges their comfort or ego. Jonah teaches us that obedience isn't about agreement—it's about surrender. I've mentored men who resist change, avoid hard conversations, or refuse to forgive. One said, "I know what I should do—I just don't want to." Jonah teaches us that obedience isn't about agreement—it's about surrender. And that God's grace is bigger than our grudges.

Peter was passionate, loyal, and bold. He walked on water and declared Jesus as the Messiah. But he also denied Jesus three times out of fear (Luke 22). His strength was zeal; his weakness was inconsistency. Men today often struggle with being one person in public and another in private. Peter's restoration by Jesus (John 21) shows that failure doesn't disqualify—it refines. I've met men who feel like frauds—strong in public, but afraid in private. One confessed, "I talk about faith, but I'm scared to live it." Peter's restoration by Jesus is one of the most tender moments in Scripture. It shows that failure doesn't disqualify—it refines. And that love restores what shame tries to bury.

Paul was a Pharisee who hunted Christians. But after encountering Jesus on the road to Damascus, he became the greatest missionary in history (Acts 9). His strength was passion; his weakness was pride. Many men today carry guilt from past mistakes. Paul's life proves that redemption is real—and that your worst chapter can become your greatest testimony. I've worked with men who carry deep regret—abortion decisions, broken families, criminal records. One said, "I don't think God can use someone like me." Paul's life proves otherwise. Redemption is real. Your worst chapter can become your greatest testimony.

Thomas is known for doubting the resurrection. He needed to see and touch Jesus to believe (John 20). His strength was honesty; his weakness was skepticism. Men today wrestle with faith, especially in seasons of loss or uncertainty. Thomas reminds us that doubt isn't the enemy of faith—it's often the doorway to deeper belief. I've met men who wrestle with faith—who want to believe but feel stuck in skepticism. One told me, "I want to trust God, but I've been disappointed too many times." Thomas reminds us that doubt isn't the enemy of faith—it's often the doorway to deeper belief. Jesus didn't shame him—He invited him closer.

Timothy was Paul's spiritual son, gifted and faithful. But he struggled with fear and needed encouragement to lead boldly (2 Timothy 1:7). His strength was loyalty; his weakness was timidity. Young men today often feel inadequate, unsure of their voice or role. Timothy's story shows that mentorship matters—and that courage can be cultivated. I've mentored young men who feel inadequate—who compare themselves, question their calling, and shrink back. One said, "I don't think I'm ready to lead." Timothy's story shows that courage can be cultivated, and that mentorship matters. Sometimes, all a man needs is someone to say, "You've got this."

Each of these men faced real struggles—temptation, failure, fear, regret. But each also encountered grace, growth, and purpose. Their stories are not just ancient history—they're mirrors. They reflect the journey every man is on to rise, to fall, to learn, and to lead.

If you're a man reading this and you see yourself in one of these stories, take heart. You're not alone. You're not beyond redemption. You're part of a long line of men who've wrestled with weakness and found strength in God.

The men of the Bible weren't saints in the way we often imagine. They were flawed, impulsive, insecure, and sometimes reckless—just like us. They made choices that hurt others, sabotaged their own futures, and left them drowning in regret. And yet, their stories are preserved—not to shame them, but to show us that redemption is possible. Their lives mirror our own. The same temptations, failures, and emotional battles they faced are the ones we wrestle with today.

Some of us stand silently while our world unravels. We don't speak up when it matters. We let someone else lead, and when things fall apart, we blame everyone but ourselves. We've avoided conflict, disengaged from our families, and refused to take responsibility. We say, "I didn't know what to do," or "It's not my fault." But silence is a choice. And passivity leaves a trail of broken trust. That story reminds us that leadership begins with presence, not perfection.

Some of us have obeyed God against all odds. We've built something meaningful, something that saved lives. But when the pressure lifted, we collapsed. We turned to alcohol, lost control, and exposed our shame. We've been pillars in our communities but drink ourselves to sleep. We say, "I'm tired. I just need to shut off." Addiction doesn't always start with rebellion—it often starts with exhaustion. And even the strongest among us need recovery.

Some of us were promised greatness, but fear made us lie. We've manipulated situations to protect ourselves, even when it hurt others. We've cheated on our taxes, hidden our addictions, or lied to our spouses. We've said, "I didn't want to lose everything, so I lied." But fear-based decisions always cost more in the long run. That story teaches us that trust in God's timing is better than control through deception.

Some of us have led others but couldn't control our temper. We've lashed out, broken things, and missed out on blessings. We've screamed at our kids, punched walls, or exploded under pressure. We've said, "I hate how I react, but I don't know how to stop." Anger is often a mask for deeper pain. And unless it's addressed, it will sabotage everything we build.

Some of us love God deeply but let lust take over. We've seen something we wanted and took it—no matter the cost. We've had affairs, watched porn in secret, or chased fantasy instead of intimacy. We've said, "I feel like I'm living two lives." Sexual brokenness isn't just about desire—it's about disconnection. But that story shows us that repentance is possible, and that God doesn't discard the broken—He restores us.

Some of us started with wisdom but ended in compromise. We had everything—wealth, influence, respect—but slowly drifted. We began with passion and purpose but lost focus. We chased success, relationships, or comfort, and forgot who we are. We've said, "I used to be on fire for God. Now I just feel numb." That story warns us that finishing well matters more than starting strong.

Some of us stood boldly for truth, but when fear hit, we ran. We isolated ourselves, begged to disappear, and forgot our purpose. We've felt burned out, depressed, and ready to quit. We've said, "I feel invisible. Like I don't matter." Even spiritual giants need rest. That story reminds us that God meets us in our lowest moments—not with judgment, but with gentleness.

Some of us have run from our calling. We didn't want to forgive, didn't want to change, didn't want to obey. We've resisted growth, avoided hard conversations, and held grudges. We've said, "I know what I should do—I just don't want to." That story teaches us that surrender isn't weakness—it's wisdom. And that God's grace is bigger than our pride.

Some of us are bold in public but afraid in private. We've made promises we couldn't keep and denied the truth when it mattered most. We've felt like imposters—strong on the outside, but full of fear inside. We've confessed, "I'm terrified of being exposed." That story shows us that failure doesn't define us. Restoration is real. And love can rebuild what shame tries to destroy.

Some of us have violent pasts. We've hurt people, made enemies, and lived with deep regret. But when grace found us, everything changed. We've been in prison, broken families, or lived with guilt for decades. We've said, "I don't think I deserve a second chance." But that story proves that redemption is possible. That our worst chapter can become our greatest testimony.

Some of us have doubted everything. We've needed proof, needed answers, needed to see for ourselves. We've wrestled with faith—wanting to believe but feeling stuck. We've said, "I've been disappointed too many times to trust again." That story reminds us that doubt isn't the enemy of faith—it's often the beginning of deeper belief. And that God doesn't shame our questions—He welcomes them.

Some of us are young, gifted, and full of potential—but afraid. We've needed someone to remind us of who we are. We've felt inadequate, compared ourselves, and shrunk back. We've said, "I don't think I'm ready to lead." That story shows us that courage can be cultivated, and that mentorship matters. Sometimes, all we need is someone to say, "You've got this."

These stories are not just ancient—they are alive. They speak to every one of us who's ever felt lost, ashamed, angry, addicted, or afraid. They show us that failure isn't final, that grace is available, and that transformation is possible.

Chapter Nineteen

POSITION

There comes a time in every man's life when he must decide whether he will simply exist or truly take his place. Not just in his career or ambitions—but in his home, his family, his church, and his community. Too many men drift through life without ever stepping into the role they were created for. They become passive observers, letting others lead, letting circumstances dictate their direction, and letting their influence fade. But manhood isn't about being present—it's about being positioned.

I've met men who are physically in the home but emotionally absent. They provide, they protect, but they don't engage. Their wives feel alone. Their children feel unseen. One father told me, "I'm always working for them, but I don't know how to be with them." Taking your position means more than paying bills—it means being a source of wisdom, strength, and emotional safety. It means listening, praying, showing up, and being the kind of man, your family can lean on—not just financially, but spiritually and emotionally.

In the family, a man's role is foundational. He sets the tone. He models love, discipline, and grace. But many men grew up without that example. They're trying to lead without ever having been led. I've walked with husbands who say, "I don't know how to be a good man—I never saw one." That's where intentionality comes in. You don't have to repeat the past. You can rewrite it. You can be the man your children will one day thank. You can be the husband your wife feels safe with. You can be the brother, uncle, or son who brings peace instead of pressure.

In the church, men often take a back seat. They assume leadership is for pastors, elders, or someone more "spiritual." But the truth is, every man has a role in the body of Christ. Whether it's serving, mentoring, praying, or simply being consistent, your presence matters. I've seen churches where women carry the spiritual weight while men remain silent. One young man told me, "I don't feel qualified to lead." But leadership isn't about perfection—it's about availability. Scripture says in 1 Corinthians 16:13, "Be watchful, stand firm in the faith, act like men, be strong." That's not a call to dominance—it's a call to responsibility.

In the community, men are needed more than ever. Not just as workers or voters, but as mentors, coaches, and examples. I've seen neighborhoods transformed because one man decided to invest in young people. I've seen schools change because one father showed up. I've seen broken systems challenged because one man refused to stay silent. Proverbs 29:2 says, "When the righteous thrive, the people rejoice." Your integrity, your courage, your consistency—it creates ripple effects. You don't have to be famous to be influential. You just have to be faithful.

Taking your position also means confronting your fears. Fear of failure. Fear of rejection. Fear of not being enough. I've mentored men who say, "I'm afraid I'll mess it up." And I always tell them: you probably will. But that's not the point. The point is to show up anyway. To lead anyway. To love anyway. Because your presence, even imperfect, is better than your absence.

It means rejecting passivity. Refusing to let life happen to you. Refusing to let your family drift. Refusing to let your faith grow cold. Refusing to let your community decay. It means standing up, speaking out, and stepping in. Not with arrogance, but with humility. Not with control, but with conviction.

It means embracing your identity. As a man created in the image of God. As a leader, a protector, a provider, a servant. It means living out Micah 6:8: "He has shown you, O man, what is good. And what does the Lord require of you? To act justly, to love mercy, and to walk humbly with your God." That's your position. That's your calling.

If you're a man reading this and you've been drifting, I want you to know it's not too late. You can take your place. You can rise. You can lead. You can love. You can be the man your world needs.

There's a man I know—let's call him Marcus—who spent years working long hours to provide for his family. He was respected at work, known for his discipline and drive. But at home, he was a ghost. His wife felt like a single parent. His kids stopped asking him to play. And when his teenage son started acting out, Marcus didn't know how to respond. He told me, "I thought I was doing everything right. I didn't realize I was missing everything important." Marcus had taken his position as a provider, but not as a father. And when he finally began showing up—emotionally, spiritually, relationally—his home began to heal.

Taking your position as a man in the home means more than paying bills or fixing things. It means being emotionally available. It means praying with your spouse, listening to your children, and creating a culture of safety and love. It means being the thermostat, not the thermometer—setting the tone, not reacting to it. I've seen marriages restored because a man chose to lead with humility instead of pride. I've seen children flourish because their father chose to be present instead of passive.

In the church, I've met men like Daniel, who sat in the back row for years. He believed in God but didn't believe he had anything to offer. "I'm not a preacher," he said. "I'm just a guy trying to stay afloat." But when he started mentoring younger men—just meeting for coffee, sharing his story—something shifted. He found purpose. He found community. And those young men found a role model. Taking your position in the church doesn't mean standing on a stage. It means standing in the gap. It means being a spiritual anchor in a world that's drifting.

In the community, I think of Jamal, a single father who started volunteering at a local youth center. He didn't have much money, but he had time. He began coaching basketball, helping with homework, and listening to kids who had no one else. "I just wanted to be the man I needed when I was their age," he told me. Jamal didn't wait for permission—he took his position. And his presence changed lives.

But not every man steps into his role easily. Some feel disqualified by their past. Others are paralyzed by fear. I remember talking to a man named Steve who had been divorced twice and estranged from his children. "I've failed too many times," he said. "I don't think I deserve to lead." But leadership isn't about perfection—it's about redemption. Steve began writing letters to his kids, showing up at church, and rebuilding his life one conversation at a time. His story reminds us that it's never too late to take your position.

There are men who struggle with passivity—who let life happen to them instead of shaping it. They avoid hard conversations, delay decisions, and hope someone else will lead. One man told me, "I just want peace. I don't want to stir things up." But peace without truth is just silence. And silence creates confusion. Taking your position means speaking when it's hard, standing when it's costly, and loving when it's inconvenient.

There are men who struggle with identity—who don't know what it means to be a man. They've been told to be tough, but not tender. Strong, but not sensitive. They've learned to suppress emotion, avoid vulnerability, and chase success. But true manhood is found in balance. In strength and softness. In courage and compassion. In leadership and listening.

Scripture calls men to rise. In Ezekiel 22:30, God says, "I looked for someone among them who would build up the wall and stand before me in the gap... but I found no one." That verse haunts me. Because too often, the gap is empty. The wall is broken. And the man is missing. But it doesn't have to be that way.

Taking your position means being the man who stands in the gap. For your family. For your church. For your community. It means showing up, speaking truth, and living with integrity. It means embracing your role—not with arrogance, but with humility. Not with control, but with conviction.

Being the best version of yourself doesn't start with achievement—it starts with character. It's not about how much you earn, how many people admire you, or how well you perform. It's about who you are when no one's watching. It's about the quiet decisions, the unseen sacrifices, and the daily discipline to live with integrity.

I once sat with a man named Robert who had built a successful business, owned a beautiful home, and was admired by many. But he confessed to me, "I feel hollow. I've built everything except myself." He had chased success but neglected his soul. His marriage was strained, his kids felt distant, and his faith was dry. Robert's story is not uncommon. Many men climb ladders only to realize they're leaning against the wrong wall.

To be the best man you can be, you have to start with humility. Humility isn't weakness—it's strength under control. It's the ability to admit when you're wrong, to ask for help, to listen more than you speak. Proverbs 11:2 says, "When pride comes, then comes disgrace, but with humility comes wisdom." Humility opens the door to growth. Pride slams it shut.

Pride is the enemy of progress. It tells you that you don't need advice, that you're always right, that vulnerability is weakness. I've seen pride destroy marriages, split churches, and isolate men from the very people who could help them. One man told me, "I didn't want to admit I was struggling. I thought I had to be strong." But strength without honesty is just a mask. And masks eventually crack.

Killing pride means choosing truth over image. It means saying, "I messed up," instead of, "It's not my fault." It means asking your wife, "How can I love you better?" It means telling your kids, "I'm sorry for how I reacted." It means confessing your struggles to a trusted friend or mentor. James 4:6 reminds us, "God opposes the proud but gives grace to the humble." If you want grace, you have to lay down your pride.

Integrity is the fruit of humility. It's being the same man in every room. It's doing what's right even when it's costly. It's keeping your word, honouring your commitments, and living with transparency. I've met men who shine in public but crumble in private. One said, "I'm exhausted from pretending." Integrity frees you from pretending. It allows you to live whole, not split.

To shine as a man of integrity, you have to do the inner work. You have to confront your wounds, your insecurities, your habits. You have to ask hard questions: What am I hiding? What am I afraid of? What am I avoiding? You have to invite God into those places. Psalm 139:23–24 says, "Search me, God, and know my heart… See if there is any offensive way in me, and lead me in the way everlasting." That's the prayer of a man who wants to shine from the inside out.

I've seen men transform—not because they got richer or more respected, but because they got honest. They started showing up for their families. They started serving in their churches. They started mentoring young men. They started living with purpose. And their lives became a light.

Being the best person you can be isn't about being perfect. It's about being present. Being real. Being humble. Being faithful. It's about showing up every day and saying, "I'm here. I'm willing. I'm growing."

If you're a man reading this and you've been chasing image over substance, I want you to know: you can change. You can grow. You can lead. You can love. You can shine—not because you're flawless, but because you're faithful.

Chapter Twenty

THE HERO

Every man has a version of himself he hasn't met yet. A stronger, wiser, more grounded version. Not perfect, but purposeful. Not flawless, but faithful. That version isn't found in the mirror—it's forged in the fire. In the decisions you make when no one's watching. In the battles you fight that no one else sees. In the quiet moments when you choose growth over comfort.

Being a hero doesn't mean becoming someone else. It means becoming who you were meant to be. It means shedding the layers of fear, shame, pride, and insecurity that have kept you stuck. It means looking at your life—not with regret, but with resolve. You can't change your past, but you can shape your future. And that starts with finding the hero in yourself.

I remember talking to a man named Chris who had spent most of his life trying to live up to other people's expectations. He was the "good son," the "reliable employee," the "quiet husband." But inside, he felt invisible. "I've never really asked myself what I want," he said. "I've just been surviving." Chris's story is common. Many men live reactive lives—responding to pressure, fulfilling roles, but never stepping into purpose. Finding the hero in yourself means asking, "What was I made for?" and daring to answer.

The hero in you isn't loud. He doesn't need applause. He shows up when you choose integrity over convenience. When you forgive instead of retaliate. When you speak truth even when your voice shakes. When you stay when it's easier to walk away. I've seen men become heroes not by saving the world, but by saving their marriage. By breaking generational cycles. By showing up for their kids. By choosing sobriety. By choosing faith.

Becoming a hero requires humility. You have to admit where you've fallen short. You must own your mistakes. You have to stop blaming others and start building yourself. Proverbs 24:16 says, "Though the righteous fall seven times, they rise again." The hero in you isn't the man who never falls—it's the man who keeps getting up.

It also requires vision. You must see beyond your current circumstances. You must believe that your life can be more than survival. That your story can be more than struggle. Jeremiah 29:11 reminds us, "For I know the plans I have for you… plans to prosper you and not to harm you, plans to give you hope and a future." That promise isn't just for the perfect—it's for the willing.

I've met men who found their hero in the middle of addiction. One man told me, "I hit rock bottom, but that's where I found my foundation." He started attending recovery meetings, rebuilding trust, and mentoring others. His past didn't disqualify him—it equipped him. I've seen men find their hero after divorce, after bankruptcy, after failure. The hero isn't born in success—it's revealed in struggle.

Finding the hero in yourself also means embracing discipline. You can't grow without structure. You need routines that feed your soul, habits that build your character, and boundaries that protect your peace. One man I coached started waking up early to pray, journal, and exercise. "It's not about being perfect," he said. "It's about showing up for myself." That's heroism—consistency in the face of chaos.

It means living with courage. Courage to confront your wounds. Courage to pursue healing. Courage to dream again. Courage to love deeply. Courage to lead boldly. 2 Timothy 1:7 says, "For God has not given us a spirit of fear, but of power and of love and of a sound mind." That power is already in you. You just have to activate it.

There's a man inside you that you haven't met yet. He's stronger than your fears, wiser than your past, and more capable than your doubts. He's not waiting for the perfect moment—he's waiting for your permission. The hero in you isn't found in applause or achievement. He's found in the quiet decision to rise when everything in you wants to quit.

I've sat across from men who've lost everything—marriages, careers, reputations—and still found a way to rebuild. One man, after a public scandal, told me, "I thought my life was over. But losing everything forced me to find myself." He started journaling, attending therapy, reconnecting with his kids, and volunteering at a shelter. He didn't become a hero overnight. But every day he chose honesty over hiding, humility over pride, and service over shame. That's what heroism looks like.

Being a hero doesn't mean becoming someone else. It means stripping away the layers of fear, ego, and comparison that have kept you from your true self. It means asking hard questions: What am I running from? What am I afraid to feel? What am I pretending doesn't hurt? The hero in you is born when you stop performing and start healing.

I've met men who've spent years chasing validation—through money, sex, status, or control—only to feel emptier with every win. One man said, "I've got the house, the car, the job. But I feel like a stranger in my own skin." That's because the better you isn't built on possessions—it's built on purpose. And purpose begins with presence. With showing up for your life, your relationships, you're calling.

To be a hero you must confront your shadows. The anger you've buried. The addictions you've justified. The wounds you've ignored. You have to stop blaming your father, your ex, your boss, your past. You have to own your story. Not with shame, but with strength. Because the hero in you doesn't deny the pain—he transforms it.

I think of a man named Eli who grew up in a violent home. His father was abusive, his mother was silent, and he learned early to protect himself by shutting down. As an adult, Eli struggled with intimacy. He couldn't trust, couldn't feel, couldn't connect. But one day, he broke. He cried for the first time in years. He started therapy. He joined a men's group. He began to forgive—not just others, but himself. And slowly, the hero emerged. Not the tough guy, but the tender warrior. The man who could feel and still lead.

You can't grow without structure. You need habits that build you, not break you. You need to wake up with intention, move your body, feed your mind, and guard your soul. One man I coached started waking up at 5 a.m. to pray, read, and walk. "It's not about being perfect," he said. "It's about showing up for myself." That's heroism—consistency in the face of chaos.

And you need courage. Courage to speak the truth. Courage to say no. Courage to love again. Courage to dream again. Courage to lead when you feel unqualified. 2 Timothy 1:7 says, "For God has not given us a spirit of fear, but of power and of love and of a sound mind." That power is already in you. You don't need to earn it—you need to activate it.

The hero in you isn't found in a moment—it's built over time. In the way you treat your spouse. In the way you show up for your kids. In the way you handle failure. In the way you forgive. In the way you serve. The better you are forged in the fire of everyday choices.

If you're a man reading this and you feel stuck, tired, or unsure of who you are, I want you to know: the hero is still in there. He's not waiting for perfection. He's waiting for permission. You don't have to be fearless. You just have to be willing.

You were made for more. Not more applause—but more impact. Not more control—but more courage. Not more image—but more integrity.

CHAPTER TWENTY : THE HERO

Chapter Twenty-One

THE CHAMPION

There's a difference between a hero and a champion. The hero rises in a moment. The champion rises every day. The hero responds to a crisis. The champion builds a life. The hero may be celebrated for one act of courage. The champion is remembered for a lifetime of consistency.

Embracing the champion in yourself means choosing discipline over impulse. It means showing up when you don't feel like it. It means doing the hard things—having the hard conversations, making the hard decisions, and staying the course when others quit. Champions aren't born in comfort. They're forged in discomfort. In the gym. In the prayer closet. In the quiet hours when no one's cheering.

I think of a man named Andre who battled depression for years. He had every reason to give up—failed relationships, financial setbacks, and a deep sense of isolation. But one day, he made a decision. He started walking every morning. Then journaling. Then reading

Scripture. Then volunteering. "I didn't feel like a champion," he said. "But I acted like one until I started believing it." That's the shift. You don't wait to feel strong—you choose to act strong. And strength follows.

Champions live with conviction. They know who they are and what they stand for. They don't chase approval—they chase purpose. They don't bend to pressure—they rise under it. I've seen men walk away from toxic relationships, turn down unethical promotions, and speak truth in rooms full of compromise. Not because it was easy—but because it was right. That's what champions do. They choose integrity over popularity.

Champions also carry resilience. Life will hit you. You'll lose people. You'll face betrayal. You'll fail. But the champion in you doesn't stay down. He learns. He adapts. He grows. Romans 5:3–4 says, "We rejoice in our sufferings, knowing that suffering produces endurance, and endurance produces character, and character produces hope." That's the champion's path—pain to perseverance to purpose.

And champions lift others. They don't just rise—they raise. They mentor. They encourage. They protect. They serve. I've seen men become champions not by winning battles, but by helping others win theirs. One man I know started a weekly breakfast with young men in his neighborhood. No agenda—just presence. "I want them to know they matter," he said. That's championship living. It's not about being the strongest—it's about being the most faithful.

To embrace the champion in yourself, you have to silence the voices that say you're not enough. The voice of your past. The voice of comparison. The voice of fear. You must replace them with truth. With Scripture. With affirmations. With the voice of God saying, "You are my son. I am pleased with you." (Matthew 3:17)

You also must surround yourself with other champions. Men who challenge you, sharpen you, and call you higher. Proverbs 27:17 says, "As iron sharpens iron, so one man sharpens another." Champions aren't built in isolation. They're built-in community.

You must carry yourself like a champion. In how you walk. How you speak. How you treat others. How you handle pressure. Not with arrogance—but with quiet confidence. Not with bravado—but with grace. The champion in you doesn't need to prove anything—he just needs to be present.

One of the most powerful things a man can do is learn to appreciate himself—not for what he's achieved, but for who he's becoming. Too many men walk through life with their heads down, weighed by guilt, comparison, and the pressure to be more. They celebrate others but never themselves. They give grace to everyone but themselves. They keep striving, but never stop to say, "I'm proud of me."

Appreciating yourself isn't vanity—it's sanity. It's recognizing the battles you've fought, the storms you've survived, the growth you've earned. It's looking in the mirror and seeing not just flaws, but progress. I've met men who've overcome addiction, rebuilt broken families, started over after failure—and still struggle to feel worthy. One man told me, "I've changed so much, but I still feel like I'm not enough." That's the lie many men live under. That no matter how far they've come, it's never enough.

But here's the truth: you are enough. Not because you've arrived, but because you're showing up. Because you're trying. Because you're growing. Philippians 1:6 says, "He who began a good work in you will carry it on to completion." That means your story isn't finished—but it's already valuable.

Appreciating yourself means celebrating the small wins. The days you didn't quit. The moments you chose patience over anger. The times you apologized, forgave, or stayed when it was easier to walk away. It means acknowledging your effort, not just your outcome. One man I coached started keeping a "daily courage list"—three things he did each day that required strength. "It helps me see that I'm not just surviving," he said. "I'm growing."

It also means speaking kindly to yourself. Many men have an inner critic that never sleeps. It tells them they're weak, stupid, lazy, or broken. But that voice isn't truth—it's trauma. It's the echo of past wounds, unmet expectations, and cultural pressure. You have to replace that voice with one of grace. With affirmations like, "I'm learning," "I'm healing," "I'm worthy of love." Proverbs 18:21 says, "The tongue has the power of life and death." That includes the tongue in your own head.

Appreciating yourself means investing in yourself. Not just financially, but emotionally and spiritually. It means taking care of your body, your mind, your soul. It means going to therapy, taking a break, reading a book, joining a group, or simply resting. It means treating yourself like someone you value—not someone you tolerate.

I've seen men transform when they start honouring themselves. They walk taller. Speak clearer. Love deeper. Not because they became perfect—but because they stopped punishing themselves. One man said, "I used to think self-love was soft. Now I know it's strength." That shift changes everything.

You can't lead others well if you don't love yourself well. You can't give what you don't have. Appreciation fuels confidence. Confidence fuels courage. And courage fuels impact.

As a champion you must first learn to appreciate yourself—not for what you've accomplished, but for who you are. That means recognizing your worth, even when no one else sees it. It means honouring the image of God within you, even when you feel broken or inadequate. Appreciation isn't arrogance; it's acknowledgment. It's saying, "I matter. I was created with purpose. I am not an accident." When you begin to see yourself through the eyes of your Creator, you stop chasing validation and start walking in identity.

Loving yourself is the next step. Not in a self-centered way, but in a way that reflects the love God has for you. Jesus said, "Love your neighbor as yourself," which implies that self-love is foundational. You can't pour into others from an empty cup. Loving yourself means forgiving your past, being patient with your growth, and speaking kindly to your own soul. It means caring for your body, guarding your heart, and nurturing your spirit. It's not about perfection—it's about compassion. Champions aren't those who never fall; they're those who rise with grace.

Living like a walking example of Jesus is where everything comes together. Jesus was the ultimate champion—not because He conquered kingdoms, but because He conquered sin, shame, and death. He walked with humility, loved with boldness, and served with joy. To live like Him means to lead with integrity, to speak truth with love, and to carry peace wherever you go. It means being strong without being harsh, being confident without being proud, and being faithful even when it's hard. Champions reflect Christ—not just in public, but in private. In how they treat others, how they handle failure, and how they respond to pain.

The Bible gives us examples of men who embodied these truths. David, though flawed, appreciated the heart God gave him. He wrote songs of worship, poured out his emotions, and never stopped seeking God's presence. He loved himself enough to repent, to fight for his people, and to rise again after failure. Joseph, betrayed and forgotten, still held onto his identity. He didn't let bitterness define him. He lived with integrity, forgave those who hurt him, and became a leader who saved nations. Paul, once a persecutor, became a champion of grace. He embraced his transformation, loved deeply, and lived every day as a reflection of Christ's mercy.

These men weren't perfect, but they were powerful. Not because of their strength, but because of their surrender. They appreciated who God made them to be, they loved themselves enough to grow, and they lived as walking testimonies of redemption. That's what makes a champion—not applause, but alignment. Not fame, but faithfulness. When we learn to see ourselves as God sees us, love ourselves as He loves us, and live as He calls us to live, we don't just win—we inspire others to rise too.

You are not a failure. You are a fighter. You are not broken. You are becoming. You are not behind. You are building.

Appreciate yourself. Honour your journey. Celebrate your growth.

Chapter Twenty-Two

UNDERSTANDING YOURSELF

To become a better man, you must first become an honest one. That means looking inward—not with judgment, but with clarity. It means naming your weaknesses, acknowledging your flaws, and accepting your imperfections. Not to excuse them, but to understand them. Because you can't heal what you won't face. And you can't grow if you're pretending, you're already there.

I've met men who are terrified of self-reflection. They stay busy, distracted, and emotionally distant because they're afraid of what they'll find if they slow down. One man told me, "I don't want to dig too deep. I might not like what's underneath." But the truth is, what's underneath is not your enemy—it's your starting point. Your wounds, your habits, your insecurities—they're not signs of failure. They're invitations to grow.

Understanding yourself means asking hard questions: Why do I react the way I do? Why do I avoid certain conversations? Why do I feel the need to prove myself? Why do I struggle with intimacy, trust, or vulnerability?

These questions aren't comfortable—but they're necessary. Because every man has blind spots. Every man has triggers. Every man has patterns. And until you name them, they'll keep running your life from the shadows.

I think of a man named Jordan who had a habit of withdrawing whenever conflict arose. His wife felt abandoned, his kids felt confused, and he felt ashamed. "I just shut down," he said. "It's how I survived growing up." Once he understood that his silence was a defense mechanism—not a character flaw—he began to change. He started speaking up, staying present, and rebuilding trust. His weakness didn't disappear overnight, but it stopped controlling him.

Coming to terms with your imperfections doesn't mean settling—it means surrendering. It means saying, "This is where I am, but it's not where I'll stay." It means giving yourself grace without giving yourself excuses. It means owning your story without being owned by it.

Striving for perfection isn't about being flawless—it's about being faithful. It's about showing up every day with a heart that's willing to grow. Matthew 5:48 says, "Be perfect, therefore, as your heavenly Father is perfect." That word "perfect" in the original Greek—*teleios*—means complete, mature, whole. God isn't asking you to be without error. He's calling you to be whole. To be integrated. To be aligned in heart, mind, and action.

I've seen men transform when they stop hiding from themselves. When they stop pretending to be strong and start becoming strong. When they stop chasing approval and start pursuing authenticity. One man said, "I used to think being a man meant never showing weakness. Now I know it means facing it."

Understanding yourself also means recognizing your strengths. Your resilience. Your creativity. Your loyalty. Your capacity to love. Too often, men focus only on what's broken. But you are more than your flaws. You are more than your failures. You are a masterpiece in progress.

To strive for perfection is to live with intention. To wake up each day and ask, "How can I be more whole today?" It's not about comparison—it's about commitment. It's not about image—it's about integrity.

Every man wears multiple hats—father, husband, son, brother, friend, leader, provider, protector. And each role carries weight. Not the kind that crushes you, but the kind that shapes you. The kind that builds muscle in your soul. The kind that reminds you that your life matters—not just for what you do, but for who you are to others.

Bettering yourself means showing up in those roles with intention. It means asking, "What kind of father am I becoming?" "What kind of husband am I choosing to be?" "What kind of man do my children see when they look at me?" These aren't questions of guilt—they're questions of growth. Because your roles aren't just responsibilities—they're opportunities. Opportunities to lead with love, to serve with strength, and to model what integrity looks like in real time.

I've met men who felt overwhelmed by their responsibilities. One man, a father of four, told me, "I feel like I'm failing every day. There's always something I didn't do." But when we looked closer, he was doing more than he realized. He was present. He was consistent. He was trying. And that effort—imperfect as it was—was shaping his children's view of manhood. Sometimes, bettering yourself means recognizing that consistency is more powerful than perfection.

In marriage, bettering yourself means learning to love sacrificially. Not just with words, but with actions. It means listening when you'd rather fix. It means staying when you'd rather escape. It means choosing empathy over ego. I've seen marriages restored not by grand gestures, but by daily humility. One husband said, "I started asking her how she was doing—and actually listening." That small shift changed everything. Because love isn't loud—it's faithful.

In friendship, bettering yourself means being dependable. Showing up. Checking in. Offering support without needing credit. I've seen men become anchors in their friend groups simply by being consistent. One man said, "I'm not the loudest guy, but I'm always there." That's what real friendship looks like—presence over performance.

In leadership—whether in your workplace, church, or community— bettering yourself means leading with integrity. It means making decisions that reflect your values, not just your goals. It means treating people with respect, even when it's inconvenient. It means owning your mistakes and modeling accountability. I've worked with leaders who said, "I want to be the kind of man my team can trust." That's the mark of true leadership—not authority, but authenticity.

Bettering yourself also means managing your responsibilities with wisdom. It means setting boundaries, prioritizing what matters, and refusing to be ruled by urgency. It means saying no to distractions so you can say yes to purpose. One man I coached started blocking out time each week for his family, his faith, and his personal growth. "I used to let my calendar control me," he said. "Now I control it." That shift gave him clarity—and peace.

And most importantly, bettering yourself means remembering that your roles are not just tasks—they're sacred trusts. Your children don't need a perfect father—they need a present one. Your spouse doesn't need a flawless partner—they need a faithful one. Your community doesn't need a superhero—they need a servant.

Colossians 3:23 says, "Whatever you do, work at it with all your heart, as working for the Lord." That includes parenting, marriage, friendship, leadership. Every role you carry is a chance to reflect God's heart. To bring light into dark places. To build something that lasts.

Bettering yourself is not just about improvement—it's about discovery. It's the process of understanding who you truly are, what you carry within, and what God has placed in your life to fulfill. When we commit to growth, we're not chasing perfection; we're stepping into purpose. We begin to see that our struggles, our strengths, and even our setbacks are part of a larger story—a divine blueprint designed for fruitfulness, impact, and legacy.

Understanding yourself means slowing down enough to listen to your inner life. It means asking hard questions: What am I afraid of? What do I believe about myself? What patterns do I keep repeating? It's in that honest reflection that clarity begins to form. You start to recognize the gifts God has given you, the wounds He wants to heal, and the calling He's inviting you to walk in. Growth is not just about doing more—it's about becoming more. It's about aligning your life with the destiny God has already written for you.

Success in God's eyes isn't measured by status or wealth—it's measured by faithfulness, fruitfulness, and obedience. When you better yourself, you're preparing to carry the weight of your calling. You're learning discipline, humility, and resilience. You're becoming someone who can be trusted with influence, someone who can lead with compassion, and someone who can endure with grace. You're not just achieving goals—you're becoming an achiever in the kingdom sense: someone who bears fruit that lasts, someone who multiplies goodness, and someone who reflects the heart of God in every season.

The Bible is filled with men who walked this journey. Take Caleb, for example. He wasn't the loudest voice in the crowd, but he was one of the few who saw the Promised Land and believed it could be taken.

While others were overwhelmed by fear, Caleb understood who he was and who his God was. He didn't let the opinions of the majority shape his identity. He stood firm, even when it meant waiting decades to see the fulfillment of God's promise. Caleb's life teaches us that when we better ourselves—by strengthening our faith, sharpening our courage, and refusing to settle—we position ourselves to inherit what God has already prepared.

Then there's Bezalel, the craftsman chosen to build the tabernacle. He wasn't a prophet or a warrior, but he was filled with the Spirit of God, with wisdom, understanding, and skill. Bezalel's story reminds us that growth isn't always loud—it can be quiet, creative, and deeply spiritual. He understood his gifts and used them to serve a holy purpose. In bettering himself, he didn't chase status; he embraced excellence. And through that, he helped shape the sacred space where God would dwell among His people.

Consider Nehemiah, a man who started as a cupbearer but became a leader and a builder. He saw a broken city and felt a burden to restore it. He prayed, planned, and persevered. Nehemiah didn't wait for someone else to fix the problem—he stepped into it. His growth came through action, through facing opposition, and through staying faithful to the vision God gave him. Nehemiah teaches us that when we understand our calling and commit to growth, we become agents of restoration in a world that desperately needs it.

There's also Josiah, a young king who inherited a kingdom full of idolatry and compromise. Instead of following the patterns around him, he sought the truth. When the Book of the Law was found, Josiah tore his robes in repentance and led his people back to God. His story shows that growth often begins with humility—with the willingness to admit we've drifted and the courage to change course. Josiah didn't let his youth or his environment define him. He chose to better himself by aligning with God's Word, and through that, he transformed a nation.

And let's not forget Mordecai, who stood firm in his convictions even when it meant risking his life. He didn't bow to pressure, and he didn't chase recognition. He mentored Esther, guided her with wisdom, and played a key role in saving his people. Mordecai's story reminds us that growth includes standing for what's right, investing in others, and trusting God's timing. He didn't seek greatness, but greatness found him because he lived with integrity.

Each of these men—Caleb, Bezalel, Nehemiah, Josiah, Mordecai—shows us that bettering ourselves is not about becoming someone else. It's about becoming who we were always meant to be. It's about understanding our identity, embracing our gifts, and walking boldly into the destiny God has prepared. When we commit to growth, we don't just change—we align. We bear fruit. We succeed in the ways that matter most. And we become living testimonies of what it means to be an achiever in God's kingdom.

These men didn't arrive fully formed. They were shaped over time—through surrender, through struggle, and through obedience. They chose to better themselves not for applause, but for alignment. They understood that to fulfill God's destiny, they had to become the kind of men who could carry it. And so must we.

When we invest in our growth, we're not just improving—we're preparing. We're saying yes to the future God has for us. We're choosing to be fruitful, to succeed in what matters, and to become achievers who leave a legacy of faith, courage, and love. This journey isn't easy, but it's holy. And every step forward is a step deeper into who we were always meant to be.

You cannot pour from an empty cup. You cannot give what you don't have. And you cannot love others well if you don't first learn to love yourself. Not in a self-indulgent, ego-driven way—but in a grounded, grace-filled, honest way. Loving yourself is the beginning of every healthy relationship you'll ever have. It's the root of empathy, patience, and connection.

If you're a man reading this and you feel stretched thin, I want you to know you're not alone. And you're not failing. You're growing. You're learning. You're becoming. Bettering yourself isn't about doing more—it's about being more. More intentional. More present. More aligned with who you were created to be.

So take a breath. Take your place. Take your role seriously—not with pressure, but with purpose.

Chapter Twenty-Three

THE HEART VS. THE HEAD

There's a difference between knowing and feeling. Between thinking and believing. Between logic and conviction. Many men live from the head—calculating, analyzing, rationalizing. They make decisions based on what's safe, what's expected what's logical. But the best version of you isn't found in cold calculation—it's found in courageous conviction. In living from the heart.

Living from the heart means being emotionally honest. It means acknowledging what you feel, not just what you think. It means saying, "I'm hurt," "I'm afraid," "I care," instead of hiding behind silence or sarcasm. I've met men who've built walls around their hearts because they were taught that emotions are weakness. One man said, "I was raised to believe that crying makes you soft." But vulnerability isn't weakness—it's strength. It's the doorway to connection, healing, and authenticity.

Living from the heart also means leading with passion. It means pursuing what matters—not just what pays. It means loving deeply, serving boldly, and showing up fully. When you live from the heart, you stop settling. You stop chasing second best. You stop living someone else's version of success. You start asking, "What sets my soul on fire?" and then you build your life around that answer.

Living from the heart doesn't mean ignoring reality. It means facing it with courage. It means living with facts—not fantasy. Too many men live in denial. They pretend their marriage is fine, their health is strong, their finances are stable—when deep down, they know something's off. One man told me, "I kept telling myself everything was okay until it all collapsed." That's the danger of fantasy—it feels good until it costs everything.

Living with facts means being honest about where you are. It means checking your bank account, your blood pressure, your emotional health, your spiritual life. It means asking, "What's really going on?" and refusing to lie to yourself. Because truth is the foundation of transformation. You can't fix what you won't face.

And once you face the facts, you strive for the best. Not comfort. Not average. Not "good enough." You push for excellence. You aim for greatness. You refuse to settle. I've seen men turn their lives around simply because they stopped accepting mediocrity. One said, "I realized I was living at 60%—and I was built for more." That shift changed everything.

Mental toughness isn't about being emotionless—it's about being resilient. It's about pushing through discomfort, staying focused under pressure, and refusing to quit when it gets hard. I've worked with men who've trained their bodies but neglected their minds. They could lift weights but couldn't lift their own self-worth. One said, "I can run ten miles, but I can't sit still with my thoughts." That's why mental toughness matters—it's the strength to face yourself.

Developing mental toughness means building habits that stretch you. Reading when you'd rather scroll. Praying when you'd rather sleep. Confronting when you'd rather avoid. It means choosing discipline over distraction. One man started waking up at 4:30 a.m. to train his mind before his day began. "It's not about the time," he said. "It's about the mindset." That mindset made him unstoppable.

Mental toughness also means managing your emotions. Not suppressing them—but mastering them. It means feeling anger without exploding. Feeling fear without retreating. Feeling sadness without drowning. It means being emotionally agile—able to feel deeply and still move forward.

Victimhood is a trap. It tells you that life is happening to you, not through you. It convinces you that you're powerless, that your past defines you, that your pain is permanent. I've met men who've been through hell—abuse, betrayal, loss—and still chose to rise. One said, "I didn't choose what happened to me, but I choose what happens next." That's power. That's freedom.

Refusing to live as a victim means taking ownership. Of your choices. Your healing. Your future. It means saying, "I may have been knocked down, but I'm not staying down." It means rewriting your story—not erasing the pain but redeeming it.

Romans 8:37 says, "In all these things we are more than conquerors through Him who loved us." That's not just a verse—it's a declaration. You are not a victim. You are a warrior. You are not broken beyond repair. You are being rebuilt. You are not stuck. You are rising.

There comes a point in every man's life when pretending becomes exhausting. When the image he's projecting no longer matches the man he's becoming. When the pressure to perform, impress, or fit in starts to suffocate the soul. That's when the real work begins—the work of becoming real.

Being real means dropping the mask. The one you wear at work. The one you wear at church. The one you wear with your friends. It means showing up as you are—not as who you think people want you to be. I've met men who've spent years curating a persona—strong, successful, unshakable—while quietly falling apart inside. One man told me, "I've built a life that looks great from the outside, but I don't recognize myself anymore." That's the cost of inauthenticity: disconnection from your own soul.

Being genuine means speaking truth. Not just facts, but feelings. It means saying, "I'm struggling," "I'm afraid," "I need help," without shame. It means being honest about your story—your failures, your doubts, your dreams. I've seen men find freedom not through perfection, but through confession. One said, "The moment I told the truth, I felt lighter." That's what truth does—it liberates.

Being true means living in alignment. Between your values and your actions. Between your beliefs and your behaviour. Between your public life and your private life. It means refusing to compartmentalize. Refusing to be one man at home and another in the world. It means integrity—not just in what you do, but in who you are.

I've seen marriages heal when a man chooses to be real and function from their heart. He stops pretending everything's fine. He starts sharing his fears, his failures, his hopes. He becomes emotionally available. And that vulnerability builds trust. I've seen friendships deepen when a man stops performing and starts connecting. He stops competing and starts listening. He stops hiding and starts showing up.

Being real also means embracing your humanity. You're not a machine. You're not a brand. You're a man—with emotions, needs, and imperfections. And that's okay. You don't have to be the strongest in the room. You just have to be the most honest. That's where real strength lives—in truth, not in toughness.

Jesus modeled this kind of authenticity. He wept. He got tired. He asked questions. He showed emotion. He lived with integrity. He didn't pretend to be someone He wasn't. And He didn't ask us to, either. In John 8:32, He said, "Then you will know the truth, and the truth will set you free." That includes the truth about yourself.

There's a difference between knowing you matter and believing it. Between hearing you're valuable and living like you are. Many men walk through life with a quiet ache—a sense that they're not enough. Not successful enough. Not strong enough. Not spiritual enough. They measure their worth by their income, their performance, their relationships, or their past. And when those things falter, so does their sense of self.

But your value isn't earned—it's intrinsic. It's not based on what you do—it's based on who you are. You were created with purpose, intention, and dignity. Psalm 139:14 says, "I praise you because I am fearfully and wonderfully made." That's not poetry—it's identity. You are not an accident. You are not disposable. You are not replaceable.

Accepting your self-worth means rejecting the lies that have shaped your self-image. Lies that say you're too broken, too late, too weak, too flawed. Lies that came from childhood wounds, failed relationships, or cultural expectations. One man told me, "I've spent my whole life trying to prove I'm not a disappointment." That kind of striving is exhausting. And unnecessary. Because your worth isn't up for debate—it's already settled.

It also means embracing your uniqueness. Your personality. Your story. Your voice. You don't have to be like anyone else to be valuable. You don't have to fit a mold to be meaningful. I've seen men come alive when they stop comparing and start accepting. One said, "I used to hate how sensitive I was. Now I see it as a gift." That shift—from shame to strength—is what self-worth looks like.

Accepting your value also means setting boundaries. You stop tolerating disrespect. You stop overextending yourself to earn approval. You stop shrinking to make others comfortable. You start saying no when it's right. You start protecting your peace. You start honouring your time, your energy, and your emotional health.

And you start showing up differently. With confidence. With clarity. With calm. Not arrogance—but assurance. Not dominance—but dignity. When you know your worth, you stop chasing validation. You stop performing. You start living.

I've seen men transform when they finally accept their value. They become better fathers—not because they're perfect, but because they're present. They become better husbands—not because they never fail, but because they love from a place of wholeness. They become better leaders—not because they have all the answers, but because they lead with authenticity.

Self-worth also fuels resilience. When you know you matter, you don't give up easily. You don't crumble under criticism. You don't retreat when life gets hard. You rise. You adapt. You endure. Because you know your life has weight. Your voice has power. Your presence has impact.

Life doesn't come wrapped in perfection. It comes in pieces—some beautiful, some brutal. The good days fill us with gratitude. The bad days test our faith. And the ugly days—those are the ones that shape us. The heartbreaks. The betrayals. The failures. The moments we didn't think we'd survive. But here's the truth: you don't become a better man by avoiding pain. You become one by walking through it and choosing to grow.

I've met men who've lost everything—jobs, marriages, health—and still chose to live with purpose. One man, after a devastating divorce, started volunteering at a local shelter. "I needed to do something that reminded me I still mattered," he said. That act of service didn't erase his pain, but it gave it meaning. It turned his brokenness into a bridge for others.

Taking the good, the bad, and the ugly means refusing to be defined by any one season. It means learning from the hard times, celebrating the good ones, and trusting that even the ugly moments can be redeemed. Romans 8:28 reminds us, "And we know that in all things God works for the good of those who love Him." Not some things—all things. Even the ones that hurt.

Making the best of life isn't about pretending everything's fine. It's about choosing to live with intention. To wake up each day and ask, "How can I make this count?" It's about finding joy in small things—a quiet morning, a kind word, a moment of connection. It's about refusing to waste time on bitterness, resentment, or regret.

Living from the heart instead of the head means shifting from survival to authenticity. It's a change in posture—from overthinking and self-protection to vulnerability and courage. When we live from the head, we often try to control outcomes, avoid pain, and calculate our worth based on performance or approval. But when we live from the heart, we begin to trust, to feel, and to show up as our true selves. It's not weakness—it's strength. It's the kind of strength that doesn't need to pretend, defend, or dominate. It's the strength that comes from knowing who you are and whose you are.

This shift requires mental toughness. Not the kind that numbs emotion or powers through pain, but the kind that faces reality with resilience. It means refusing to be a victim of circumstance, even when life has been unfair. It means choosing growth over bitterness, truth over denial, and healing over hiding. Mental toughness is the ability to hold both joy and sorrow, to keep going when it hurts, and to believe that your story still matters. It's not about being hard—it's about being whole.

To live this way, we must accept our self-worth. Not the version shaped by comparison or criticism, but the worth that comes from being made in the image of God. You are valuable—not because of what you've done, but because of who you are. Accepting yourself means embracing the good, the bad, and the ugly. It means owning your story, forgiving your failures, and celebrating your progress. It means being real, genuine, and true—even when it's uncomfortable.

The Bible gives us examples of men who made this shift. Take Jephthah, for instance. He was rejected by his family, cast out because of his mother's reputation, and forced to live on the margins. He could have stayed bitter, defined by rejection. But when his people needed a leader, he stepped up. He didn't let his past disqualify him. He led with courage, and though his story is complex, it shows a man who chose purpose over pain.

Then there's Asa, a king who started strong by tearing down idols and leading his people back to God. He lived from conviction, not convenience. But later in life, he relied more on strategy than on faith. When faced with conflict, he leaned on alliances instead of prayer. His story reminds us that living from the heart is a lifelong choice. It's easy to drift back into the head—into control, fear, and pride. But the heart calls us to trust again.

Another example is Baruch, Jeremiah's scribe. He wasn't a prophet or a warrior, but he carried the weight of truth in a time of chaos. He struggled with discouragement, even despair. But God spoke to him directly, reminding him that his life had purpose beyond recognition. Baruch's story teaches us that living from the heart means accepting that your role may be quiet, but it's still sacred. It means finding peace in obedience, not applause.

We also see this in Eleazar, one of David's mighty men. In battle, when others fled, he stood his ground. He fought until his hand froze to his sword. That kind of grit doesn't come from the head—it comes from the heart. From a place of deep conviction, loyalty, and courage. Eleazar didn't fight for glory—he fought because he believed in something worth defending.

Living from the heart is not easy. It asks us to feel deeply, to risk vulnerability, and to walk in truth. But it's the only way to live fully. When we stop overthinking and start trusting, when we stop hiding and start healing, we become the kind of men who change the atmosphere around us. We become grounded, present, and powerful—not because we have it all together, but because we're willing to be real.

This is the path to becoming whole. To move from victimhood to victory. To develop mental toughness that's rooted in grace. To accept our worth, embrace our story, and live with open hearts. It's not just a mindset—it's a way of being. And it's the way we were always meant to live.

CHAPTER TWENTY-THREE : THE HEART VS. THE HEAD

Chapter Twenty-Four

THE MATH

Every man is a builder. Whether he realizes it or not, he's constructing something with his life—his character, his legacy, his relationships, his faith. And like any builder, he must constantly evaluate the materials he's using. What are you adding to your life? What are you taking away? What are you subtracting that no longer serves you? What are you dividing to multiply your impact?

As men, we are constantly adding to our lives—layer by layer, moment by moment. Whether we realize it or not, every decision, every challenge, and every relationship is shaping who we are becoming. We are not static beings. We are evolving, growing, and refining. The question is not whether we are changing, but what we are choosing to carry with us. What values are we embracing? What strengths are we cultivating? What principles are we standing on? These are the building blocks of our identity, and they determine the kind of legacy we leave behind.

Values like integrity, humility, and compassion don't just appear—they are chosen. They are forged in the quiet moments when no one is watching. Strength is not just physical—it's emotional, spiritual, and moral. It's the ability to stand firm when the winds of life blow hard. Abilities are not just talents—they are the skills we develop through discipline, curiosity, and perseverance.

Concepts like grace, justice, and stewardship shape how we see the world and how we treat others. Principles like honesty, loyalty, and courage become the compass that guides our decisions. Character is the sum of all these things—it's who we are when everything else is stripped away. Personality adds colour to our presence, and reflection gives depth to our journey.

In the Bible, we see men who added these elements to their lives with intention and faith. Take Elisha, for example. He wasn't born a prophet—he was called into it. When Elijah threw his cloak over him, Elisha didn't hesitate. He left everything behind and followed. But he didn't just inherit a title—he pursued the spirit and character of his mentor. He asked for a double portion, not out of pride, but out of purpose. Elisha added boldness, obedience, and spiritual sensitivity to his life. He became a man of miracles, not because he was perfect, but because he was prepared.

Another example is Benaiah, one of David's mighty warriors. He wasn't the most famous, but his story is unforgettable. He chased a lion into a pit on a snowy day and killed it. He faced giants and came out victorious. Benaiah added courage, fearlessness, and loyalty to his life. He didn't wait for safety—he stepped into danger with faith. His character earned him a place as the head of David's bodyguard, a position of trust and honour. He teaches us that strength is not just about muscle—it's about mindset.

We also see this in Ezra, the scribe and priest who led a spiritual revival. He didn't just know the law—he lived it. He prepared his heart to seek the Lord, to do His will, and to teach others. Ezra added wisdom, discipline, and devotion to his life. He didn't chase influence—he cultivated depth. His leadership brought clarity and conviction to a people who had lost their way. Ezra reminds us that intellectual and spiritual growth go hand in hand.

Then there's Obed-Edom, a man whose home became the resting place of the Ark of the Covenant. He didn't resist it—he welcomed it. And because of his reverence, his household was blessed. Obed-Edom added hospitality, honour, and spiritual awareness to his life. He didn't seek greatness, but greatness found him because of his posture. His story shows us that sometimes what we add to our lives is not loud—it's sacred.

These men weren't perfect, but they were intentional. They chose to add depth, strength, and truth to their lives. They didn't settle for survival—they pursued significance. And so must we. As men, we are called to be more than reactive—we are called to be reflective. To ask ourselves, "What am I building? What am I carrying? What am I becoming?" The answers to those questions shape our identity, our relationships, and our legacy.

We add to our lives every time we choose forgiveness over resentment, discipline over distraction, and truth over convenience. We grow when we face our fears, own our mistakes, and lean into grace. We become more when we stop performing and start transforming. This is the journey of manhood—not just to exist, but to evolve. Not just to succeed, but to serve. Not just to be strong, but to be whole.

To grow as a man, you must add what strengthens you. Add wisdom through Scripture. Add discipline through routine. Add peace through prayer. Add courage through community. Add love through service. These are the nutrients of manhood. Without them, you'll starve spiritually and emotionally.

I've seen men transform simply by adding one new habit—daily journaling, morning prayer, weekly mentorship. One man said, "I started reading Proverbs every day. It changed how I speak, how I lead, how I think." That's the power of addition. Small inputs, big outcomes.

Add truth. Add accountability. Add grace. Add time with people who challenge you to be better. Add silence when the world gets loud. Add purpose to your calendar. Add value to every room you enter.

As men, part of our growth is not just about what we add to our lives, but what we subtract. Subtraction is a sacred act. It's the intentional removal of what no longer serves us—habits, mindsets, behaviours, and patterns that keep us stuck, small, or bitter. It's the pruning that makes room for fruit. When we subtract addiction, we reclaim clarity. When we subtract negativity, we make space for hope. When we subtract comparison, we rediscover our unique path. Subtraction is not loss—it's liberation.

We subtract weakness not by pretending to be strong, but by facing what makes us fragile and choosing to heal. We subtract toxic temperaments by learning emotional regulation, by refusing to let anger or pride dictate our responses. We subtract the nagging and complaining by cultivating gratitude, by choosing to speak life instead of draining it. These aren't easy shifts. They require honesty, humility, and a willingness to change. But every time we subtract what's harmful, we strengthen what's holy.

The Bible gives us examples of men who chose subtraction as a path to transformation. Take Hezekiah, a king who inherited a nation steeped in idolatry and spiritual decay. He didn't continue the cycle—he broke it. He tore down the high places, smashed the sacred stones, and reopened the temple. He subtracted compromise and restored worship. His story shows us that leadership sometimes means removing what's familiar to make room for what's faithful.

Another example is Manasseh, Hezekiah's son, who started with rebellion but ended with repentance. He built altars to false gods, practiced sorcery, and led Judah astray. But when he was taken captive, he humbled himself and cried out to God. He subtracted pride, arrogance, and rebellion—and God restored him. Manasseh's story reminds us that it's never too late to subtract what's destroying us. Even the most toxic patterns can be uprooted when we surrender.

We also see this in Zacchaeus, the tax collector who climbed a tree to see Jesus. He was known for greed and exploitation, but one encounter changed everything. He didn't just add generosity—he subtracted dishonesty. He gave back what he had stolen, multiplied his restitution, and walked away from a life of manipulation. Zacchaeus teaches us that subtraction is often the first step toward redemption.

Another man worth noting is Naaman, the Syrian commander who suffered from leprosy. He came to Israel seeking healing, but almost missed it because of pride. He expected grandeur but was told to wash in the Jordan River. At first, he resisted. But when he finally let go of his ego, he received his healing. Naaman subtracted entitlement and embraced obedience. His story shows us that subtraction often requires humility before breakthrough.

Even the prodigal son, though unnamed, offers a powerful example. He subtracted his illusions of independence, his reckless living, and his pride. When he returned home, he didn't bring riches—he brought repentance. And that was enough. His subtraction made room for restoration, for celebration, and for identity to be reclaimed.

As men, we must ask ourselves: What are we holding onto that's holding us back? What attitudes, addictions, or assumptions need to be released? Subtraction is not weakness—it's wisdom. It's the decision to stop feeding what's killing us and start nurturing what's healing us. It's the courage to say, "This no longer belongs in my life," and to walk away from it, even if it's familiar.

When we subtract what's toxic, we make room for what's true. When we subtract what's heavy, we make space for what's holy. This is the work of becoming—not just better, but freer. Not just stronger, but wiser. And not just successful, but surrendered. Every man has something to subtract. And every subtraction is a step closer to the man we were always meant to be.

Growth requires subtraction. You cannot become who God called you to be while holding onto everything that's keeping you stuck. Take away bitterness. Take away pride. Take away toxic relationships. Take away excuses. Take away the need to be liked by everyone.

Subtraction is different from removal. It's about reducing the weight of what you can't fully eliminate. You may not be able to quit your job, but you can subtract the stress by setting boundaries. You may not be able to change your past, but you can subtract its power over your present.

Subtract overcommitment. Subtract emotional baggage. Subtract the need to control everything. Subtract the pressure to be perfect. One man told me, "I stopped trying to fix everyone. I started focusing on being present." That subtraction gave him peace—and gave others space to grow.

Subtract the noise. Subtract the guilt. Subtract the fear of failure. Because when you lighten the load, you walk with more freedom.

As men, part of our growth involves learning to divide wisely. Division is not about separation—it's about discernment. It's the ability to distinguish what belongs where, what needs priority, and what must be released. We divide our time, our energy, our focus, and our emotions so that we can live with balance, clarity, and purpose. Without healthy division, everything blurs together—work invades family, desires override responsibilities, and the past clouds the present. But when we divide well, we create space for what matters most.

We divide work time from family time because both deserve our full attention. Our careers may demand much, but our families need our presence. It's easy to justify long hours with the promise of provision, but children remember presence more than paychecks. Our spouses need more than our leftovers—they need our intentional love, our listening ears, and our shared laughter. Dividing time well means choosing to be fully where we are, not half-present everywhere.

We also divide our own wants and desires from the needs of those we love. Marriage, fatherhood, and friendship require sacrifice. It's not about losing ourselves—it's about learning to serve. When we divide selfishness from selflessness, we become more whole. We learn to say, "What do you need?" instead of always asking, "What do I want?" This kind of division builds trust, deepens intimacy, and strengthens relationships.

There's a division between weakness and strength that every man must face. It's not about denying weakness—it's about recognizing it and choosing to grow. Strength isn't the absence of struggle—it's the courage to confront it. We divide the parts of ourselves that sabotage growth from the parts that fuel it. We name our fears, our triggers, our patterns, and we choose to rise above them. That's where resilience is born.

We divide mistakes from identity. We've all made wrong choices, but those choices don't define us. They teach us. We learn to say, "That was a mistake, not a reflection of my worth." We divide shame from growth, guilt from grace. We own our failures, but we don't live in them. We use them as steppingstones, not stumbling blocks.

And perhaps most importantly, we divide the past from the present. We honour where we've been, but we don't let it dictate where we're going. We learn to live in the now—to be present with our families, engaged in our purpose, and aware of our blessings. The past may inform us, but it must not imprison us. Division here means choosing freedom over regret.

The Bible offers examples of men who understood this kind of division. Take Jethro, Moses' father-in-law. He saw Moses overwhelmed with responsibility and taught him to divide his leadership—delegate tasks, create structure, and protect his energy. Jethro's wisdom helped Moses lead more effectively and preserve his well-being.

Another example is Boaz, a man who divided personal gain from moral responsibility. He could have ignored Ruth, a foreign widow with no status, but he chose integrity. He divided cultural norms from godly compassion and became a redeemer. His story shows that division can lead to legacy.

We also see this in Elihu, the young man who spoke in the book of Job. He waited patiently while older men spoke, but when he finally spoke, he divided emotion from truth. He brought clarity, not chaos. He didn't speak to impress—he spoke to illuminate. Elihu teaches us that division can bring wisdom when it's rooted in humility.

Another man, Ebed-Melech, an Ethiopian servant in Jeremiah's time, divided fear from courage. When Jeremiah was thrown into a cistern, Ebed-Melech risked his position to rescue him. He didn't let fear silence him. He divided comfort from conviction and chose justice.

These men weren't perfect, but they were intentional. They knew when to draw lines, when to shift focus, and when to choose what mattered most. As men today, we must do the same. We must divide wisely—not to isolate, but to prioritize. Not to fragment, but to focus. Division is a discipline. It's the art of living with purpose, of choosing what builds over what breaks, and of becoming men who lead with clarity, compassion, and conviction.

As men, we are constantly multiplying something from our lives—whether intentionally or not. Multiplication is the act of taking what we've been given and expanding it. It's not just about producing more; it's about producing meaning. We multiply our life experiences when we share our stories. We multiply our skills when we teach others. We multiply our knowledge when we apply it with wisdom. We multiply our influence when we lead with integrity. Every day, we are sowing seeds that will grow into something—either fruit or weeds. The question is: what are we multiplying, and why?

Life gives us raw material—pain, joy, lessons, victories, failures. When we choose to reflect on those experiences and use them to help others, we multiply healing. When we take the skills we've developed and pass them on, we multiply legacy. When we gain knowledge and pair it with humility, we multiply wisdom. Even power, recognition, and fame can be multiplied in healthy ways—when they're used to elevate others, not just ourselves. Multiplication is not about ego; it's about stewardship. It's about taking what's in our hands and asking, "How can this serve beyond me?"

The Bible offers examples of men who multiplied what they were given, not for personal gain, but for divine purpose. Take Elkanah, the father of Samuel. He wasn't a prophet or a king, but he was a man of devotion. He led his family in worship, honoured his wife Hannah's spiritual longing, and supported her vow to dedicate their son to God. Through his faithfulness, he multiplied spiritual legacy. Samuel became one of the greatest prophets in Israel's history, and it started with a father who understood the power of surrender.

Another example is Hur, a man who stood beside Moses during battle. When Moses' arms grew tired, Hur helped hold them up. He didn't seek the spotlight, but his support multiplied victory. His strength and loyalty contributed to a moment that changed history. Hur teaches us that multiplication doesn't always come from leading—it often comes from lifting.

We also see this in Apollos, a gifted speaker in the New Testament. He was passionate and eloquent, but he was humble enough to be taught by Priscilla and Aquila. He multiplied his effectiveness by receiving correction. He didn't let pride block growth. As a result, he became a powerful voice in the early church. Apollos reminds us that multiplication often begins with teachability.

Another man, Tychicus, served alongside Paul. He wasn't the one writing letters, but he was the one delivering them. He carried messages, encouraged churches, and supported the mission. His reliability multiplied the reach of the gospel. Tychicus shows us that multiplication can come through consistency, not just charisma.

Even the centurion who approached Jesus for healing multiplied faith. He understood authority and believed that Jesus could heal with just a word. His trust and humility became a model of faith that Jesus publicly praised. That moment multiplied understanding of spiritual authority and belief.

As men, we must ask ourselves: what are we multiplying? Are we multiplying bitterness or grace? Are we multiplying fear or courage? Are we multiplying isolation or connection? The answer lies in how we live, how we lead, and how we love. Multiplication is not just about what we do—it's about who we empower, what we leave behind, and how we show up.

When we multiply the right things—wisdom, kindness, truth, and strength—we become more than successful. We become significant. We become men who don't just build for ourselves but build for generations. That is the power of multiplication. And that is the calling we carry.

When you add what builds, take away what breaks, subtract what drains, and divide what blesses—you shine. Not with ego, but with excellence. Not with noise, but with light. Philippians 2:15 says, "Then you will shine among them like stars in the sky." That's your calling—to be a light in dark places. To live with clarity, courage, and compassion.

God didn't call you to be average. He called you to be authentic. He didn't call you to be perfect. He called you to be purposeful. He didn't call you to be popular. He called you to be powerful—in humility, in truth, in love.

So take inventory. What are you adding? What are you taking away? What are you subtracting? What are you dividing? And then—shine.

Chapter Twenty-Five

SERVING

Serving, at its core, means giving of yourself—your time, your energy, your gifts—for the benefit of others. It's not about recognition or reward; it's about reflecting the heart of God. To serve is to step into the posture of humility, to choose love over convenience, and to see others through the lens of grace. It's the daily decision to say, "I'm here for more than myself."

When we talk about serving in relation to the Unrivalled God, we're talking about aligning our lives with the One who set the standard. God is not just powerful—He is personal. He doesn't demand service from a distance; He demonstrated it up close. Jesus, God in flesh, said, "I did not come to be served, but to serve, and to give my life as a ransom for many" (Matthew 20:28). That's the model. That's the mission.

Serving the Unrivalled God means surrendering our pride, our plans, and our preferences. It means asking, "What does God want from me today?" and being willing to follow through. It's not just about church roles or ministry titles—it's about living with open hands and an open heart. Whether it's helping a neighbor, mentoring a younger man, or simply being present for your family, service is sacred.

And serving His people is how we make His love visible. The Bible is filled with men who served God by serving others. Think of Joseph, who endured betrayal and prison, yet chose to forgive and provide for the very brothers who wronged him. His service preserved a nation. Or Boaz, who protected and provided for Ruth, not out of obligation, but out of honour. His kindness became part of the lineage of Christ.

Even Paul, once a persecutor of the church, became one of its greatest servants. He travelled, preached, wrote, and suffered—all to build up the body of Christ. His letters remind us that serving is not glamorous—it's gritty. It requires endurance, compassion, and a heart fixed on eternity.

Serving also means stepping into the needs of the moment. It's being interruptible. It's choosing to listen when someone needs to talk, to help when someone's overwhelmed, and to lead when others hesitate. It's not about being perfect—it's about being available.

When we serve the Unrivalled God and His people, we become part of something eternal. We become carriers of hope, builders of peace, and reflections of divine love. And in that service, we find joy—not because it's easy, but because it's holy.

Serving the unrivalled God, means serving His people for Who He is—He stands alone—above all powers, authorities, and idols. There is no equal to His wisdom, no match for His strength, and no comparison to His love. He is the Creator of all things, the sustainer of life, and the source of truth. Unlike human leaders or fleeting philosophies, God is eternal, unchanging, and perfectly just. He doesn't compete for greatness—He defines it. Serving an unrivalled God means recognizing that our lives are not our own, and that true purpose is found in surrendering to His will.

When we serve like Him, we reflect His heart. God's way of serving is not transactional—it's transformational. He doesn't serve to gain; He serves to give. Jesus, who is God in flesh, modeled this perfectly. Though He had all authority, He washed feet. Though He could command angels, He chose a cross. His service was marked by humility, sacrifice, and compassion. To serve like Him means to lead with love, to give without expecting, and to show up even when it's inconvenient.

Serving like God means stepping into the lives of others with empathy and truth. It means listening when someone needs to be heard, helping when someone is hurting, and standing firm when someone needs protection. It's not about being perfect—it's about being present. It's about showing grace in failure, offering strength in weakness, and choosing integrity over image.

We serve like Him when we forgive those who've wronged us, when we mentor those who are searching, and when we carry burdens that aren't our own. We serve like Him when we choose kindness over comfort, truth over popularity, and faithfulness over convenience. It's not always easy, but it's always holy.

To serve an unrivalled God is to live with reverence and responsibility. It's to say, "Not my will, but Yours." And it's to let that surrender shape how we treat our families, our communities, and even our enemies. When we serve like Him, we don't just reflect His image— we reveal His presence.

Men are called to serve an Unrivalled God—the one true source of our strength. In a world that often measures masculinity by dominance, independence, or achievement, Scripture offers a radically different foundation: strength rooted in surrender. The God we serve is not one among many. He is unmatched, unshaken, and unchanging. And when we anchor our lives in Him, we find not only identity, but also the power to live with integrity, initiative, and purpose.

Unrivalled strength begins with recognizing that we are not the source of our own power. We may be capable, intelligent, and resourceful, but apart from God, our strength is limited and fleeting. Psalm 18:2 declares, "The Lord is my rock, my fortress and my deliverer; my God is my rock, in whom I take refuge." This is not poetic exaggeration—it's a declaration of dependence. Real strength is found not in self-reliance, but in divine reliance.

Consider the life of Asahel, the brother of Joab, mentioned in 2 Samuel. He was known for his speed and courage in battle, but his strength alone could not save him. He pursued Abner with boldness, yet fell because he lacked wisdom and restraint. Asahel's story reminds us that physical strength without spiritual grounding can lead to downfall. It's not enough to be fast, brave, or skilled—we must be anchored in God's wisdom and timing.

Then there's Uzziah, a king who started well. He sought God, and as long as he did, he prospered. His military campaigns were successful, his fame spread, and his leadership flourished. But when pride crept in, he entered the temple to burn incense—something only priests were permitted to do. God struck him with leprosy, and he lived the rest of his life in isolation. Uzziah's story teaches us that strength must be tempered by humility. When we forget that our success comes from God, we risk losing everything.

Men today face countless pressures—providing for families, leading in workplaces, navigating relationships, and battling internal struggles. It's easy to feel overwhelmed, inadequate, or tempted to perform. But God doesn't call us to carry the weight alone. He invites us to stand in His strength. Isaiah 40:31 says, "But those who hope in the Lord will renew their strength. They will soar on wings like eagles; they will run and not grow weary, they will walk and not be faint." This is the kind of strength that sustains—not just in moments of triumph, but in seasons of trial.

Living with integrity means choosing truth when it's costly, staying faithful when it's inconvenient, and leading with love when it's easier to withdraw. It means being the same man in private as you are in public. And that kind of consistency requires supernatural strength.

Initiative means stepping up—not waiting for someone else to lead, but being the first to forgive, to serve, to protect. Purpose means living with intention, knowing that your life is part of a bigger story.

Look at Mordecai, the cousin of Esther. He didn't have a throne or an army, but he had conviction. He refused to bow to Haman, not out of arrogance, but out of reverence for God. He mentored Esther, guided her with wisdom, and stood firm in the face of danger. Mordecai's strength came from his faith, and through it, he helped save a nation.

Men are called to be pillars—not because we are perfect, but because we are planted in something greater than ourselves. Our families need us to be steady. Our communities need us to be courageous. Our workplaces need us to be ethical. And our own souls need us to be surrendered. The Unrivalled God we serve is not distant— He is near. He is the source of every good thing we long to be.

So stand in that strength. Not in bravado, but in boldness. Not in pride, but in purpose. Let your life reflect the power of a God who never fails, never fades, and never forgets His promises. In Him, you are more than capable—you are called. You are not just a man—you are a man of God. And that makes all the difference.

Serving an Unrivalled God means more than worship, prayer, or personal devotion—it means reflecting His heart in how we treat others. The strength we receive from Him is not meant to be hoarded; it's meant to be poured out. When we serve God, we serve people. That's the divine design. The closer we walk with Him, the more we begin to see others through His eyes—with compassion, patience, and grace. True service to God always leads us outward.

Jesus made this clear when He said, "Whatever you did for one of the least of these brothers and sisters of mine, you did for me." Serving others is not a side task—it's central to our calling. It's how we embody the character of Christ. It's how we live out our strength with humility, our purpose with generosity, and our integrity with action.

Look at the life of Nehemiah. He didn't just rebuild walls—he rebuilt dignity. He served God by serving his people, leading with compassion and conviction. He listened to their cries, stood up to injustice, and worked alongside them. His leadership was rooted in prayer, but expressed through service. Nehemiah shows us that serving God means stepping into the mess, not standing above it.

Consider the story of Joseph of Arimathea. He was a wealthy man, a member of the council, yet he used his influence to honour Jesus after His death. He asked for the body, prepared the tomb, and gave generously. His service wasn't loud—it was sacrificial. He didn't serve for recognition; he served out of reverence. That's what it means to serve an Unrivalled God—quiet acts of courage that reflect divine love.

Even the deacons in Acts, like Stephen and Philip, were chosen not for their status but for their character. They served tables, cared for widows, and preached truth. Their lives remind us that serving others is not beneath us—it's the very expression of spiritual maturity. Stephen's final moments, forgiving his killers, show that serving God means loving even when it costs everything.

As men, we are called to be protectors, providers, and leaders—but not in the worldly sense. We lead by serving. We protect by listening. We provide by showing up. Our strength is not proven by dominance, but by how we lift others. Serving an Unrivalled God means choosing kindness over convenience, sacrifice over self, and presence over pride.

It means being the man who helps without being asked. The man who forgives when it's hard. The man who mentors the younger, honours the elder, and loves the broken. It means being a safe place, a steady hand, and a voice of truth. When we serve others, we're not just doing good—we're revealing God.

This is the kind of manhood that transforms families, communities, and generations. Not because we're perfect, but because we're willing. Willing to serve the Unrivalled God by serving the people He loves. That's where real strength lives. That's where purpose is found. And that's the legacy worth leaving.

The Unrivalled Mission is not just a calling—it's a way of life. It's the divine assignment given to every man who chooses to follow the Unrivalled God. This mission is not passive, not optional, and certainly not reserved for the few. It's a daily invitation to live with purpose, to walk with courage, and to serve with conviction. It's about stepping into the story God is writing and becoming a vessel through which His truth, love, and power are revealed.

To live intentionally on mission means we must first understand that we are not alone. God never calls a man without equipping him, and He never sends him without surrounding him. Empowering each other is part of the mission. Proverbs 27:17 says, "As iron sharpens iron, so one man sharpens another." We are meant to challenge, encourage, and strengthen one another. When we share our stories, our struggles, and our victories, we remind each other that the mission is worth it—and that we are not fighting alone.

Look at Barnabas, whose name means "son of encouragement." He empowered Paul when others were afraid of him. He vouched for him, walked with him, and helped launch his ministry. Barnabas didn't seek the spotlight—he helped others step into theirs. His life teaches us that empowering others is not about control—it's about calling forth greatness. When we empower each other, we multiply impact.

Being active participants in the life of the church means showing up—not just physically, but spiritually and emotionally. It means using our gifts, serving with joy, and leading with humility. Romans 12:4–6 reminds us that we are one body with many members, each with different functions. Spectators watch; participants build. The church needs men who will pray, teach, mentor, and serve—not because they're perfect, but because they're present.

Consider Silas, who travelled with Paul on missionary journeys. He was imprisoned, beaten, and yet still sang praises in the darkest places. Silas didn't just attend church—he embodied it. He lived the mission with boldness and resilience. His story shows us that participation is not about comfort—it's about commitment.

Sharing the good news of Jesus Christ with boldness and authenticity is the heartbeat of the mission. It's not about having all the answers—it's about having a real encounter with grace. Acts 4:13 says of Peter and John, "When they saw the courage of Peter and John and realized that they were unschooled, ordinary men, they were astonished and took note that these men had been with Jesus." Boldness doesn't come from credentials—it comes from connection.

Take Philip, the evangelist who met the Ethiopian eunuch on the road. He didn't hesitate. He explained the Scriptures, baptized him, and sent him on his way rejoicing. Philip's willingness to share the gospel in a personal, authentic way changed a life—and possibly a nation. His story reminds us that the mission is not confined to pulpits. It happens on roads, in homes, and in everyday conversations.

The Unrivalled Mission calls us to live with open hands and open hearts. It asks us to be men who empower, engage, and evangelize. It's not about being perfect—it's about being available. It's about saying, "Here I am, Lord. Send me." And it's about helping other men say the same.

This mission is sacred. It's urgent. And it's ours. Let's live it with intention. Let's serve with passion. Let's speak with truth. And let's walk together—brothers on a mission, empowered by grace, fueled by love, and anchored in the strength of an Unrivalled God.

Serving like Jesus means stepping into the everyday with a heart of compassion, a posture of humility, and a willingness to meet people where they are. Practical missions aren't reserved for the few—they're open to every man who's willing to say, "Here I am." Whether in the church or the community, there are countless ways to reflect the servant-hearted nature of Christ.

In the church, practical mission begins with presence. It's showing up—not just to be fed, but to feed others. Men can serve as greeters, ushers, or mentors. They can lead small groups, teach Bible studies, or help with youth ministry. They can offer their skills in maintenance, tech, music, or hospitality. Every role matters. Jesus washed feet—He didn't wait for a platform. He served in the unnoticed spaces, and that's where impact often begins.

Serving also means being available for prayer and encouragement. Men can be part of prayer teams, visit the sick, or support those grieving. They can help organize food drives, clothing donations, or outreach events. These acts of service build the body of Christ and create a culture of care. When men serve with consistency and sincerity, they become pillars in the church—steady, trustworthy, and deeply impactful.

In the community, practical mission looks like stepping outside the walls of the church and into the needs of the neighborhood. It's volunteering at shelters, mentoring at-risk youth, or helping single parents with practical tasks. It's offering rides to appointments, helping with job readiness, or simply being a listening ear. Jesus didn't wait for people to come to Him—He went to them. He walked into villages, sat at tables, and touched the untouchable.

Men can serve through coaching sports, organizing community clean-ups, or partnering with local organizations that care for the vulnerable. They can use their professional skills—whether in finance, trades, education, or counseling—to uplift others. Serving like Jesus means seeing every interaction as sacred. It's not about grand gestures—it's about faithful presence.

Scripture gives us examples of men who lived this way. Think of Ananias in Acts 9, who was called to minister to Saul after his conversion. Despite fear, he obeyed and played a key role in launching Paul's ministry. Or think of Cornelius, a Roman centurion whose generosity and prayers caught God's attention. His household became one of the first Gentile communities to receive the gospel. These men served with courage and openness, and their obedience changed history.

Serving like Jesus means being interruptible. It means choosing people over convenience, compassion over comfort, and mission over maintenance. It's not about being perfect—it's about being present. Every act of service, no matter how small, becomes a thread in the tapestry of God's kingdom.

So whether it's stacking chairs, mentoring teens, feeding the hungry, or simply showing up with a willing heart—this is the mission. And when men embrace it, they don't just change others—they are changed themselves. That's the beauty of serving like Jesus. It's not just what we do—it's who we become.

Unrivalled Calling is not just a concept—it's a divine reality waiting to be embraced. Especially on Sunday mornings, when men gather in churches across the world, there's a sacred opportunity to step into something deeper. It's more than attending a service. It's about awakening to the truth that we were created for purpose, strength, and impact. But to walk in that calling, we must first confront the hidden battles that keep us from it.

Every man faces inner struggles. Fear of failure. Fear of not being enough. Fear of being exposed. We compare ourselves to others—how they look, how they lead, how they succeed—and quietly wonder if we measure up. We carry past mistakes like invisible weights, believing they disqualify us from future purpose. We smile in public but wrestle in private. And Sunday morning, for many, becomes a place of performance rather than transformation.

But the Unrivalled Calling of God doesn't demand perfection—it invites surrender. It's not about being flawless; it's about being faithful. Faith in Christ is what frees us from the grip of insecurity. It's what silences the voice of comparison and rewrites the story of our past. In Him, we are not defined by what we've done, but by what He's done. And that changes everything.

Look at Gideon. When God called him a "mighty warrior," Gideon was hiding in a winepress, afraid and unsure. He responded with doubt: "My clan is the weakest... and I am the least in my family." But God didn't back down. He saw beyond Gideon's insecurity and spoke to his identity. Gideon's story reminds us that calling isn't based on confidence—it's based on God's commission. And when Gideon finally stepped into that calling, he led a nation to victory with only a handful of men.

Or consider Jeremiah, who said, "I do not know how to speak; I am too young." God didn't argue—He affirmed. "Do not say, 'I am too young.' You must go to everyone I send you to." Jeremiah's calling wasn't about age or ability—it was about obedience. And through his life, God spoke to kings, nations, and generations.

Peter is another example. He denied Jesus three times, failed publicly, and wept bitterly. But after the resurrection, Jesus restored him—not with shame, but with love. "Do you love me?" Jesus asked. And with each affirmation, Peter was re-commissioned. He went on to preach boldly, lead the early church, and write letters that still shape our faith today. His past didn't cancel his calling—it prepared him for it.

Practically, this means that on Sunday mornings, men must come not just to sit, but to seek. To lay down the masks and pick up the mission. It means showing up with honesty, engaging with the Word, and opening ourselves to community. It means finding a brother to pray with, a mentor to learn from, and a younger man to invest in. It means saying, "I'm not here to spectate—I'm here to serve."

It also means recognizing that our calling is not confined to the pulpit. It's in the parking lot, the coffee line, the nursery, the tech booth, the prayer room. Every space is sacred when it's surrendered. And every man has something to offer—whether it's a word of encouragement, a helping hand, or a listening ear.

Overcoming insecurity starts with truth. The truth that you are chosen. That you are equipped. That you are loved. And that your past is not your prison—it's your platform. When men begin to believe that Sunday morning becomes more than a routine. It becomes a launchpad. A place where calling is clarified, courage is cultivated, and lives are changed.

So step in. Not with fear, but with faith. Not with comparison, but with conviction. You were meant for more. And the Unrivalled God who calls you is faithful to complete the work He began in you. Let Sunday morning be the moment you say yes—not just to church, but to calling.

CONCLUSION

As we close the pages of *What Every Man Should Know – Timeless Truths for Living with Purpose, Strength, and Integrity*, we don't end a book—we mark the beginning of a deeper journey. This has not been a manual for perfection, but a mirror for reflection. It's been a call to rise, to return, and to remember who you truly are.

You've walked through the layers of identity—who we are as men—not just in title, but in truth. You've explored the sacred bonds of brotherhood and friendshiphood, the weight and wonder of fatherhood, the humility of sonhood, and the devotion of husbandhood. These roles are not burdens—they are blessings. They are not just responsibilities—they are reflections of the divine image etched into your soul.

You've faced the struggles men often hide: insecurity, social awkwardness, the ache for connection, the confusion around boundaries, the pull of sex and desire, and the pain of infidelity and onanism. You've been invited to confront these not with shame, but with grace. Not with denial, but with truth. Healing begins when honesty steps in.

You've learned that discipline and self-care are not signs of weakness, but marks of wisdom. That godly character is not built-in moments of applause, but in the quiet choices of integrity. You've been handed a blueprint—not to follow blindly, but to build intentionally. You've examined your strengths and weaknesses, your position in life, and the calling to be both hero and champion—not for ego, but for legacy.

You've been challenged to understand yourself—not just intellectually, but emotionally and spiritually. To live from the heart, where authenticity resides, rather than the head, where fear and calculation often dominate. You've embraced the math of manhood—what to add, subtract, divide, and multiply—so that your life becomes a testimony of transformation.

And above all, you've been reminded that you serve an Unrivalled God. In Him, you find strength that doesn't fade, identity that doesn't fracture, and purpose that doesn't expire. You've been called to live on mission—to empower others, to engage in the life of the church, and to share the good news of Jesus with boldness and authenticity. You've been invited to overcome your insecurities and step fully into your calling, especially on Sunday mornings when the world needs men who show up with faith, not fear.

This is not the end. It's the beginning of becoming. Becoming the man who leads with love, who lives with integrity, and who walks with purpose. You are not alone. You are not forgotten. And you are not too late. The world needs you. Your family needs you. The church needs you. And God has never stopped believing in you.

So rise. Walk forward. Live what you now know. And let your life speak of the timeless truths that every man should carry—not just in theory, but in practice. This is your moment. This is your mission. This is your manhood.